F-51 MUST
UNITS OVER KOREA

OSPREY FRONTLINE COLOUR 1

F-51 MUSTANG
UNITS OVER KOREA

Warren Thompson

First published in Great Britain in 1999 by Osprey Publishing,
Elms Court, Chapel Way, Botley, Oxford, OX2 9LP

ISBN 1 85532 917 4

Edited by Tony Holmes
Page design by Ken Vail Graphic Design, Cambridge, UK
Cutaway Drawing by Mike Badrocke

Origination by Valhaven Ltd, Isleworth, UK
Printed in Hong Kong

99 00 01 02 03   10 9 8 7 6 5 4 3 2 1

FRONT COVER *During the first 18 months of the Korean War,
the 12th Fighter Bomber Squadron (FBS) had all of its F-51s
trimmed in blue and yellow paint. Sometime in the spring of
1952, this scheme began changing to a solid yellow trim on the
wingtips and vertical stabiliser of the replacement aircraft. This
colour change was relatively insignificant, however, for it was the
famous sharksmouth that adorned each and every squadron
fighter that set the unit apart from the others in the 18th Fighter
Bomber Wing (FBW). BUTCHIE is seen here taxying out at
Hoengsong (K-46), which served as the wing's forward staging
base, loaded with GP bombs in the summer of 1952 (Ted Hanna)*

BACK COVER *Having completed his pre-flight checks,
Lt Roy E Bell glances out the cockpit before firing up the engine
in his Mustang. When Lt Bell arrived in Japan, he was initially
assigned to the 35th FBG, but he later ended up flying with the
12th FBS out of Chinhae (K-10), where this photo was taken
(Roy Bell)*

TITLE PAGE *Capt Charles Schreffler poses in his flight suit
alongside the 'main menu' of ordnance that was being 'served'
to the North Koreans by the F-51D The large shaped charges
on the head of the rocket projectiles (RPs) were highly effective
against tanks, as was the 500-lb general purpose (GP) bomb
attached to the wing pylon inboard of RPs. At the time this
was taken in 1950, the 18th Fighter Bomber Group (FBG)
was operating with two squadrons of Mustangs, namely the
12th and 67th Fighter Bomber Squadrons (FBSs) (Charles
Schreffler)*

OPPOSITE *Even with the working conditions and facilities as crude
as they were at Taegu and Pusan, the maintenance people kept a
large percentage of their aircraft mission-ready. The blue and
yellow trim of this F-51D indicates that it was from the 12th FBS
(Charles Trumbo)*

EDITOR'S NOTE

To make the new *Osprey Frontline Colour* series as authoritative
as possible, the editor would be interested in hearing from any
individual who may have relevant information relating to the
aircraft/units/pilots featured in this, or any other, volume
published by Osprey Aviation. Similarly, comments on the edito-
rial content of this book would also be most welcome. Please
write to Tony Holmes at 10 Prospect Road, Sevenoaks, Kent,
TN13 3UA, Great Britain.

Other Osprey Aviation titles include:

Frontline Colour 2:
F-86 Sabre Fighter-Bomber Units over Korea
ISBN 1 85532 929 8

Aircraft of the Aces 4:
Korean War Aces
ISBN 1 85532 501 2

Aircraft of the Aces 7:
Mustang Aces of the 3rd, 9th & 15th AF
ISBN 1 85532 583 7

Aviation Pioneers 1:
X-Planes – Research Aircraft 1891–1970
ISBN 1 85532 876 3

For a catalogue of all books published by Osprey Military,
Aviation and Automotive please write to:
**The Marketing Manager, Osprey Publishing
Limited, PO Box 140, Wellingborough, Northants
NN8 4ZA, United Kingdom**

OR VISIT OUR WEBSITE AT
http://www.osprey-publishing.co.uk

Contents

Left *Last minute details are being looked after right before this 67th FBS F-51D launches on another mission. The pilot has all of the necessary gear in his flight bag, along with maps and target co-ordinates. This strike requires only napalm, so more than likely it is against suspected enemy troop concentrations close to the frontlines. The mission was being flown out of the 18th's HQ base at Chinhae sometime in 1951 (Max Tomich)*

Introduction

The velocity with which advancing technology, and an escalating arms race, entered the early Cold War years was unprecedented. Nuclear weapons were in mass production, and the jet aircraft that were being produced by both the Soviet Union and the United States would be able to fly higher and faster than anything that had previously been in service. It seemed that as soon as a new aircraft went operational, it was already obsolete! In the late 1940s and early 1950s, it also seemed that this race was out of control.

The United States and Great Britain had a problem that the Soviets did not have to face. They had to 'sell' their general population on what they were doing. The key to being in this race was to obtain the funding, and it became a public relations side-show. The USAF was touting an all-jet fleet that was second to none, and by 1949 this image had at last reached Far East Air Force (FEAF), and its World War 2-vintage fighters were unceremoniously cast aside, to be replaced by F-80 Shooting Stars.

The most notable 'retiree' was the North American F-51 Mustang. Five short years after it had been touted as the greatest Allied fighter of World War 2, it no longer had the speed or image to survive in the USAF's frontline inventory. According to the air force's official records, at the time the Korean War began on 25 June 1950, there were a total of 764 F-51 Mustangs assigned to Air National Guard (ANG) units in the USA, and another 794 scattered across America in storage.

However, despite the fighter's acknowledged obsolescence, the first emergency call from FEAF in the immediate aftermath of the North Korean invasion was for 'more F-51s'! These were hastily assembled and shipped over to the war zone aboard USS *Boxer* (CV 21), all 145 aircraft that were sent being drawn from ANG squadrons.

On 31 May 1950, less than a month prior to the outbreak of war, FEAF possessed a total of 1172 aircraft. This figure included a large number of aircraft that were in storage in Japan and the Philippines. Indeed, of this total, only 553 were assigned to operational squadrons. These numbers were truly pitiful when compared with what had been available at the end of World War 2. Of this operational total, 365 were F-80s, 32 F-82 Twin Mustangs, 26 B-26 Invaders and 22 B-29s, along with a handful of other secondary types.

One type is glaringly missing from this 'order of battle' – the F-51 Mustang. Twenty-five days later, the FEAF would thrust into combat against a well-equipped and well-motivated North Korean military machine that only moved in one direction – south.

It should be noted that when the 'pendulum of war' swung in favour of the UN forces and, for a very brief period, it looked like the conflict would be over by Christmas, all three F-51 wings operated from captured North Korean airfields. This also applied to another World War 2 veteran, the F4U Corsair. These outdated fighters proved to be the only aircraft types to use enemy soil on an operational basis throughout the Korean War.

Warren E Thompson
Germantown, Tennessee
April 1999

Chapter One

ORGANISED CONFUSION

When the North Korean army stormed over the border into South Korea, the US armed forces found that they had an insufficient number of troops stationed in Japan to even make a dent in the communists' advance southwards. As was indicative of the postwar years in the Far East, the American military was out of shape and undermanned, both in terms of personnel and equipment – this problem afflicted all branches of the service.

Even though FEAF listed no F-51s in its active inventory, there were several that had been retained for target towing duties in Japan, and still more in storage at various air force bases (ABs) dotted across the country. Within days of the invasion these 'forgotten' aircraft would be in great demand in the wake of an order issued by HQ Fifth AF for every Mustang that was available, regardless of condition, to be made available for operations in Korea.

The first thrust into the war by the F-51 was initiated through the hastily-formed 'Bout One' Project organised by the 8th Fighter Bomber Group (FBG) at Itazuke AB, in Japan. A total of ten F-51s were rounded up by the group, most of which had been towing targets for years. These would subsequently be manned by a team of Republic of Korea Air Force (RoKAF) Mustang pilots and American instructors picked from within the 8th FBG.

On 30 June 1950, under the leadership of Maj Dean Hess, the unit moved up to Taegu to immediately commence operations. From the beginning, it was evident that the RoKAF pilots did not have the experience, or training, to handle the Mustang in a combat environment, and from that point on, all missions were flown by the experienced American pilots. The demand on these few fighters was extremely heavy. They would take off with a full load of ordnance, bombing North Korean armour and troops along the west coast, before heading east over the mountains to strafe targets that were located on the east coast.

Fifth AF Commander, Lt Gen Earle Partridge, knew that the only chance of jamming up the North Korean advance was to put as many F-51 Mustangs on South Korean soil as he could. With that in mind, he only had two options. Firstly, he had to bring every Mustang that was available in-theatre out of storage and restore their combat status. This would give him enough aircraft to put an effective Provisional Squadron in place, and perhaps even equip one frontline squadron – this would subsequently become the 40th Fighter Interceptor Squadron (FIS) of the 35th Fighter Group (FG). Secondly, he could issue a rush request to call up a large number of Mustangs from ANG ranks and ship them over on a fast aircraft carrier.

The latter portion of this order was carried out within days, and by the middle of July, 145 Mustangs had

RIGHT *Crude conditions and no hangars prevailed while early F-51 operations tried to stem the flow of enemy forces toward the southern end of the Korean peninsula. The hot and dry weather at Taegu in the high summer is clearly reflected in this panoramic view, taken in July 1950 (Duane Biteman)*

LEFT *On 15 July 1950, USS Boxer sailed from NAS Alameda, in California, for Japan. On board were 145 Mustangs taken from ANG units from all over the United States, and 70 experienced F-51 pilots. The carrier made the Pacific crossing in just eight days, and once in-theatre, the much-needed fighters were made combat ready and rushed to frontline in South Korea (Ray Carnahan)*

been flown into Naval Air Station (NAS) Alameda and loaded on the hangar and flight decks of USS *Boxer*. After an eight-day, high-speed, crossing of the Pacific, the carrier arrived in Tokyo Bay on 23 July. Also onboard were 70 pilots, most of whom had had flown the Mustang in combat during World War 2. 1Lt Lee Gomes had been flying the F-82E Twin Mustang with Strategic Air Command's (SAC) 27th Fighter Escort Wing (FEW) at Bergstrom AB, in Texas, when the call went out. He recalls those hectic days;

'There were 21 pilots selected from our wing. A C-54 flew in and picked us up for the flight to California. When we arrived on 13 July, the carrier was loaded with close to 150 Mustangs. They filled the hanger deck and most of the flight deck. It was the largest number of aircraft I have ever seen packed on a carrier deck! Also on *Boxer's* deck were 18 Navy fighter and attack aircraft. If those Navy pilots had had to launch off the deck, it would have been a one-way flight, as there wasn't enough room to recover them.

'The captain of the ship told us he was going to put the throttles at full speed and wire them in that position. He wasn't joking, because we made the crossing in eight days! About two days out, we started zigzagging in case any North Korean submarines were between us and Japan. We had no escort on the trip, as any other ship would have had a difficult time keeping up with us. While we were en route, it was assumed that the complement of pilots that had been brought over would form up a

new fighter group, and we would all stay together. The ranking officer among us, Lt Col Milton Glessner, started several training classes to review flight operations of the F-51, with a heavy emphasis placed on the armament systems and combat tactics.'

RETIRED MUSTANGS RETRIEVED

While the order had gone out to start rounding up the ANG Mustangs, steps were also being taken to retrieve those F-51s that had already been 'retired' – some 30 aircraft were brought out of various and sundry storage areas and made combat ready. The first priority for these aircraft was to form them into a provisional squadron in order to get them to Korea. On 3 July, Thirteenth AF ordered the 18th FBG, based at Clark AB, in the Philippines, to pool together a group of experienced pilots and send them to Johnson AB to fly the F-51. The nucleus of these pilots were drawn from the 12th FBS, and they would be known as the 'Dallas' Squadron.

In the meantime, Fifth AF had formed the 51st FS(Provisional) on 10 July, which duly moved to Taegu AB with authorisation to take over all of the 'Bout One' and 'Dallas' people. The 6002nd Air Base Squadron (ABS) was also established at this time in order to oversee all logistical support for the new squadron.

The 'Dallas' pilots flew their first combat sorties over South Korea on 15 July – the very day that USS *Boxer* weighed anchor at NAS Alameda and headed for Japan.

Capt Duane 'Bud' Biteman was one of the original 'Dallas' pilots, and he recalls those very early missions flown with just ten worn out F-51s;

'On my first combat mission I was scheduled to fly wing for a seasoned fighter pilot named Capt Howard "Scrappy" Johnson. Since we had a limited number of Mustangs, we flew two-ship sorties instead of the standard four-ship flights. We took off in a swirl of dust, gaining altitude and using the railroad tracks as our main navigational aid. We proceeded into the Taejon area, where we made radio contact with a T-6 "Mosquito" pilot who was returning to Taegu for fuel. He told us that anything on the road north of Taejon was all-enemy.

'We could see raging tank battles below and heavy smoke from scores of burning buildings. Three miles north of the city, we found our targets – three Soviet-built T-34 tanks on the main road. From 8000 ft, Johnson peeled off into a near vertical dive. Seconds later, I followed him. Our bombs hit about 20-30 ft from the tanks, and they survived unscathed. We then lined up for a firing pass with our rockets. From 300 yards out, we salvoed our rockets, hitting them in the treads. The hatches popped open and they began firing machine guns at us.. Since we only had our 0.50-cal ammo left, we

LEFT *Lt William 'Romeo' McCrystal was one of the pilots chosen to fly the Mustang in South Korea as part of 'Bout One' – a composite group made up of instructor pilots from the 8th FBG, plus a handful of RoKAF pilots. Hastily organised on 27 June 1950, the group immedi-ately moved 'up-country' to Taegu AB, which was little more than a crude grass and gravel strip close to the frontline. As this shot shows, some of the 'Bout One' Mustangs carried RoKAF markings (William McCrystal)*

BELOW LEFT *The 'Bout One' group was given ten F-51Ds with which to try and slow down the whole of the advancing North Korean People's Army (NKPA)! These aircraft had been towing targets in Japan for several years prior to their return to action, and were generally in a pitiful state of repair. The demand placed on this small group was heavy, and pilots often had to work over the entire width of the peninsula on the same sortie (Duane Biteman)*

moved on down the road in search of other targets.

'Just south of Suwon, we came across two trucks loaded with North Korean troops. "Scrappy" made the first pass, hitting the lead truck in its engine. The troops scattered for the surrounding ditches. We both lined up on either side of the road and made firing passes, taking out a large number of the soldiers that were in the ditches. Our machine guns were very effective against moving vehicles and troops. The second truck blew up, so we had done enough damage here. We were drawing a lot of small arms fire, but fortunately all of their rounds completely missed our aircraft. We returned to Taegu to rearm and refuel.'

The variety of ordnance available to the Mustangs was very limited, their most effective weapons proving to be napalm and the aircraft's integral 0.50-cal machine guns. The rockets that were used were stocks left over from World War 2, and due to their age they were very erratic – although proved to be good 'tank stoppers' when they impacted on the treads of the Soviet-built T-34s. In records kept by the 51st FS(P), it is noted that they also experimented with using light case 500-lb GP bombs, filled with thermite and napalm. These bombs were extremely effective against enemy tanks and troops, for the significant amount of rubber in the tank's treads would ignite, thus disabling it.

Hastily-assembled external tanks attached to the Mustang' pylons housed the napalm. In statements made by hundreds of North Korean prisoners, the weapon that was most feared was this jellied mixture of naphtha and palm oil, which ignited on impact with the ground.

During the opening weeks of the war, the Mustangs came face-to-face with numerous Soviet-built fighters that were flown by North Korean pilots. Many of these encounters provoked vicious dogfights, with American pilots reporting that their opponents were often very good. However, when the 'dust settled' in late 1950, close to 20 North Korean People's Air Force (NKPAF) fighters had been destroyed in aerial duels, or on the ground, by the F-51. Although pleased with their success, the Mustang pilots knew that they were in-theatre to attack troop columns, tanks and anything else that moved on the ground, as Lt William 'Romeo' McCrystal (one of the first F-51 pilots to fly from Taegu) confirmed;

'On each mission that we flew, our job was to destroy targets on the ground. We were allowed to dogfight only after our mission was complete, or if attacked by enemy aircraft during the course of the mission. Therefore, most of the fights we got into were started by the North Koreans, with us at a distinct disadvantage – low on fuel, altitude and, more often than not, ammo.

'In the fighter-bomber role, we were always "low and slow". But I can tell you that in flying the fighter or fighter-bomber role, it was an exciting life!'

RIGHT '*MO'S MOCHINE*' *was the mount of the most experienced combat pilots in-theatre, Maj Harry H Moreland, who served as both commanding officer of the 'Dallas' Squadron and the 12th FBS. His aircraft is shown at Taegu during the early days of the war (Harry Moreland)*

Chapter Two

35th FIGHTER GROUP

The 35th FG had been one of the USAAF's elite fighter groups of World War 2, flying P-39s, P-47s and P-51s in near-continual combat from Pearl Harbor through to VJ-Day. Some of their best work had come in the last year of the war over the Philippines and Okinawa as American forces pushed towards Japan. As a reward for this, when the occupation forces were selected following the Japanese surrender, the 35th FG was chosen to provide air defence for the general area around Tokyo.

By the time the Korean War erupted, the group had become well versed in the ways of the jet fighter, with all three of its squadrons (the 39th 40th and 41st FISs) flying Lockheed's F-80. The group was filled with experienced jet pilots, these individuals having scored high marks on the gunnery ranges in Japan just prior to the invasion.

The group also controlled the 339th All Weather Squadron (AWS), which was equipped with the awesome F-82 Twin Mustang. With the F-80 operating exclusively as a day fighter, the 339th was left to handle the air defence role during the hours of darkness.

The FEAF's frantic search for an earlier generation of 'fair weather' fighter during late June 1950 had seen such a large number of F-51s brought out of storage in the Far

East that there were enough available to stock both the new 51st FS(P) and one regular fighter squadron. Once armed with this information, Brig Gen Edward Timberlake, Deputy Commander of Fifth Air Force, made two decisions, both of which had the endorsement of his boss, Gen Earle Partridge.

The first was to bring the 35th FG's 40th FIS into the war using these 'extra' Mustangs. Secondly, he decided that the unit must utilise the old Japanese base at Pohang-do (K-3), on the southern tip of the Korean peninsula. With Taegu jammed up with the 51st FS(P), Timberlake was left with no choice but to open up a second airfield on Korean soil.

With this decision having been made, the 802nd Engineer Battalion's Company A duly loaded their equipment onto an LST and made a rapid move from Okinawa to Pohang on 10 July. Work on this run-down base began 48 hours later, with priorities given to adding a 500-ft PSP extension to the existing runway, and constructing 27 hardstands for the Mustangs.

On 10 July Gen Timberlake also informed the 40th FIS, at Ashiya AB, that they would be the first frontline Fifth AF fighter squadron to covert from the F-80 to the

RIGHT *The 40th FIS was the first regular Fifth AF squadron to be re-equipped with the F-51 Mustang, and they moved up to Pohang AB (K-3) on 16 July 1950 to commence combat operations against the North Koreans. Their aircraft were easily identifiable, with red/white spinners and red trim on the vertical stabilisers. The 40th was part of the 35th FG that had been based at Johnson AB, in Japan, pre-war (Oakley Allen)*

LEFT *Two of the 35th FG's three squadrons went from operating in the best of conditions at Johnson AB to the worst at Pohang. This photo shows the 40th FIS's emblem painted on the hanger door at Johnson AB prior to the unit's move to Korea (Walt Bryan)*

BELOW LEFT *Groundcrews prepare themselves to turn these 40th FIS Mustangs around for another mission as they taxy up with all ordnance expended. The only protection from the elements on offer at Pohang were tents, as seen in the background to the right of this photo. The distance to the targets shrunk each day as the North Korean advance continued (Ray Stewart)*

BELOW *To protect themselves during daylight hours, large groups of North Korean troops would often hide in some of the South Korean villages – especially when the Fifth AF had any of their aircraft operating in the area. This napalm attack was carried out by 39th FIS Mustangs (Dick Penrose)*

F-51. Six days later, the 40th flew their newly-acquired fighters into Pohang and immediately commenced combat operations.

On 30 June the United Nations' war efforts got a major boost when the Australian Ambassador announced that his country was releasing No 77 Sqn, with its full complement of Mustangs, to the control of UN forces. The Royal Australian Air Force (RAAF) had maintained a major base at Iwakuni since the occupation of Japan, and the 'Aussies', with their 26 aircraft, would subsequently be attached to the 35th FG until they converted onto Meteor F 8s in 1951. However, No 77 Sqn did not officially come under 35th control until 12 October, and prior to this date, they maintained their HQ at Iwakuni AB, although they often flew joint missions with both the 39th and 40th FISs.

WEATHER RESTRICTIONS

Although the invasion of South Korea had taken place at the start of summer, the weather in the area still had a tendency to turn bad with very little notice. Rain and low overcasts in July had hampered operations, especially over mountainous terrain.

Poor flying weather often had little effect on the war on the ground, however, and when the 40th FS got embroiled in its own 'little war' with a large force of 1500+ North Korean regulars, pilots were forced to fly in extremely marginal conditions. The NKPA troops were using the coastal road down from Yonghae in an attempt

to capture Pohang, and the only force standing in their way was a single RoKAF regiment, backed up by a squadron of ageing F-51s.

Pilots eventually became oblivious to the low ceiling of 150 ft as they mounted numerous sorties day after day. It became a personal battle, and captured NKPA soldiers stated that most of their transportation had been knocked out by the low flying Mustangs. They also claimed that their commanding officer had notified his superiors that unless he was reinforced, he could not take Pohang. The squadron averaged over 34 sorties per day during the battle for Pohang, and it was this effort that prevented the base from falling into enemy hands. The efforts of the 40th FIS graphically illustrated Gen Partridge's point when he said that in order to be successful in stopping the enemy, he had to have F-51s operating from bases in South Korea, and not Japan.

The arrival of *Boxer* with its cargo of F-51s allowed FEAF to disperse a large number of these aircraft to various squadrons, and at last form an effective force to oppose the North Korean advances. It was quickly decided to convert the 40th FIS's sister unit, the 39th FIS, from the F-80 back to the Mustang – this transition had been completed by 7 August. The next day, the squadron moved up to Pohang to join the 40th, thus raising the 35th FG's fighting force to two squadrons.

For those FEAF aircraft that were having to launch and recover out of Japan, missions over Korea were a test of both flying skills and endurance. It didn't make any difference whether you were flying a jet or a piston-engined aircraft, the crossing over the Sea of Japan soon 'got old'. On the one hand you had all the creature comforts at bases in Japan, but on the other hand you were home quicker, and avoided that long overwater stint in a single-engined aircraft, if you were based in Korea – but the conditions were as crude as one could imagine.

Lt Marvin Wallace, a pilot in the 39th FIS, saw action from bases in Korea in the early days. Seeing combat in both the F-80C and the Mustang, he was happy to trade creature comforts for shorter missions;

'Soon after we got our F-51s we moved over to Pohang. The living conditions at Ashiya were equivalent to those found at a stateside air base – good quarters, offi-cers club, a theatre, swimming pool, chapel etc. Pohang had none of that. We lived in tents whose only source of heat was a pot-bellied stove in the middle, and our food came out of cans.

'But, even with these conditions, I was glad to make the move. It was about 120 miles across the Korea Strait, so that flying out of Japan meant an hour over water, each way. Most of the guys that went down over this stretch with battle damage were never found. I once saw a school of large fish (sharks) down there when I was forced to descend to about 50 ft because of low clouds. My old Mustang was purring, so I wasn't worried, but just knowing there were several hundred sharks in water below me

LEFT *By March 1951 the battle lines had stabilised, although the Chinese were still nightly running hundreds of trucks south loaded with supplies in an attempt to support the launch of a major new offensive against UN forces. The F-51s were working overtime at this point, trying to disrupt the truck convoys. These two RAAF Mustangs, and a 39th FIS F-51D, are rearming assembly line style at Suwon, which was being used as a major Mustang staging base at the time (Lloyd Johnson)*

added a little zest to the crossings. I could readily accept a field toilet at Pohang-do to avoid that crossing everyday!'

There is an old saying that it is the darkest right before dawn. The North Koreans must have quickly learned this because they started moving transports on the roads just prior to 'sun up'. The enemy knew that the daylight hours belonged to the Mustang pilots, who could seriously disrupt their movements. The 40th FS soon realised what was going on, and modified their mission pattern, as Lt Wallace recalls;

'We were going to try and get the jump on some of the enemy trucks by hitting them at first light, before they could pull over and hide. This was a pre-dawn launch, and there was some heavy equipment working on a taxyway near the far end of the runway. This added an element of risk to the take-off. Our flight leader tried to call the tower twice to get some runway lights turned on, but got no response either time. So we just took off with our landing lights on and a full load of ordnance onboard! If we had developed trouble and had to turn around, we could not have found the darkened runway.

'Anyway, we caught the enemy convoy completely off guard and torched all of their equipment with napalm. I could make out the dim figures of troops taking cover in a nearby river bed. There were countless twinkles of light coming from amongst them as they fired their rifles at us. I did not take any hits, but one of the Mustangs in my flight had six holes in its fuselage. We took a chance on getting up to them in total darkness, but it was certainly worth it because we caused a lot of damage.'

One of the many unusual stories to come out of those early days was told by Lt Walt Bryan, one of the provisional group pilots at Taegu who flew with the 40th FIS during those early days. It involved one of the true heroes to come out of the Korean War, Maj Gen William F Dean, commander of the 24th Division. Bryan recalls the strange events of 15 July 1950;

'That morning I flew my 13th mission of the war. Immediately after landing, I was summoned over to report to Gen Partridge and Maj Hess. They informed me that a runway control jeep was being loaded on a C-47 for Taejon, and I was to accompany it. I thought to myself that one minute I was a fighter pilot and the next I was a forward air controller (FAC) working in "no man's land"!

'Upon landing at Taejon, I immediately reported in to the 24th Division HQ and Gen Dean. Over the next few days I found myself in a desperate fight for survival. We were doing everything from calling in fighter strikes to directing artillery fire. The Mustangs and F-80s responded quickly to our calls, but there was just so much they could do to stop the crushing momentum that the enemy had. We would set up road blocks, but the enemy just went around them. The division had so many killed and

RIGHT *By the Spring of 1951 the 40th FIS was having a hard time keeping a full complement of Mustangs mission-ready. The unit had been grossly overworked over the past few months, and by this stage of the war it wasn't expecting any replacement aircraft. This photo of a war-weary F-51D was taken at the forward staging base at Suwon (K-13) (Lloyd Johnson)*

wounded that it was a wonder they could put up any resistance. At this point, Gen Dean ordered me out of Taejon and over to Oakchon. It was important to save this taxi jeep, with its precious radio equipment!

'Soon after I moved one of my fellow 40th pilots, flying an L-19, dropped me a clean pair of overalls. Unfortunately for me, they were many sizes too big. Right after I had put them on, Gen Dean drove up in his jeep and noticed my clothes. Grinning, he stated that it appeared that my clothes were too big, and that his fatigues were too small, so why didn't we swap out, and we did. This was an unusual exchange between a 1st lieutenant and a major general, but true! This was the last time I saw the general. He was cut off by the enemy and evaded for 30 days before being captured. We made it out, barely, and hooked up with the 1st Cavalry Division. Gen Dean became one of the highest ranking PoWs of the war. From that time on, when flying a mission over our troops, it took on an entirely different meaning.'

Although the 40th FS launched most of its missions from its Pohang-do base on the southern tip of Korea, they also staged numerous times from Suwon and Kimpo, before recovering back to their main base. For the most part, these missions were flown after the frontlines had stabilised in early 1951.

SKIP-BOMBING

During the Spring of 1951, the unit got into the routine of hunting down trucks and trains that might have been damaged during night attacks by Marine nightfighters and USAF B-26s. 1Lt Lloyd Johnson recalls a mission that saw him pull off a very successful skip-bombing attack using 500-lb GPs;

'We were working pretty close with some of the B-26 night intruders. One night they claimed they chased a train into a tunnel, and they thought it would still be there after first light. We got the location and figured it would be in one of two tunnels in the area.

'I took one of the tunnels and worked out a route to get the best angle on the entrance. I made my run and dropped both bombs at the same time. They had delay fuses on them which prevented detonation for between five and eight seconds after hitting the ground. The right bomb went wide and hit a few feet off the opening, but the left one skipped right in the tunnel, and about six seconds later all hell broke loose. At first, a ring of smoke came out of the entrance, followed by several massive secondary explosions. The tunnel wasn't very long, so evidently the locomotive was pulling only a few cars loaded with munitions. The bomb probably had time to skip under the trailing car before exploding, and the entire train went up. It was a mission that I will always remember!'

By the Spring of 1951, the massive Chinese offensive had bogged down due to the lack of supplies, thus firming up the frontline. The F-51 had contributed significantly to undermining the communists' supply train, but the attrition rate on these hard-working aircraft had in turn been very heavy. By April, there were not enough Mustangs available in-theatre, to outfit all of the squadrons, so something had to give On 25 May the 35th FG was transferred back to Japan to assume their original tasking of air defence. The 40th FIS moved to Misawa AB, on northern Honshu, and sister-squadron the 39th took what was left of their F-51 inventory and joined up with the 18th FBW as an attached squadron. Their new bases would be at Chinhae (K-10) and Hoengsong (K-46), in southern Korea.

Chapter Three

8th FIGHTER BOMB GROUP

Like the 35th FG, the 8th was another combat-seasoned fighter group that had made a name for itself during World War 2 in the Pacific. When the war ended, the group was also chosen to become part of the Occupation Forces, being based on the western end of Japan, with its HQ at Itazuke AB. When the Korean War began, they were the first to answer the call, and their F-80s accounted for most of the aerial 'kills' made during the first few days of the conflict. Indeed, their attached all-weather F-82 squadron, the 68th, shot down the first enemy aircraft of the war. Unlike their sister group, the 35th, they would retain their F-80s for a longer period of time, thus becoming the last group to convert back to the F-51.

The 8th FBG was comprised of three squadrons – the 35th, 36th and 80th FBSs. When the call came to give up their F-80s for Mustangs, the 80th 'Headhunters' retained their Shooting Stars, whilst the 35th and 36th

made the transition. Fully equipped with Mustangs by 11 August, the two 8th FBG units became the fifth and sixth frontline fighter squadrons within the Fifth AF to revert back to the F-51.

The war was now exactly 46 days old, and Gen Partridge ordered that all of his Mustangs would be used to support the ground troops. The F-80s, meanwhile, would be utilised to fly sweeps north of the frontline in an effort to cut communications and supply movements. The loiter time of the F-51 was a tremendous asset for Forward Air Controllers, for it gave them time to pinpoint and prioritise targets while the fighter-bombers 'stacked up' and waited for orders. This could not have been achieved so effectively with the F-80 due to its limited endurance.

In the largest amphibious landings since D-Day, the 1st Marine Division came ashore at Inchon (Operation *Chromite*), south-west of Seoul, on 15 September 1950

BELOW *36th FBS CO, Lt Colonel William O'Donnell, poses by his F-51 after a long mission over enemy territory. His Mustang was easily identified by the three red command stripes painted around the rear fuselage (William O'Donnell)*

and pushed inland. The Marines' advance swiftly broke the back of the NKPA, and in a matter of hours the enemy was in full retreat northwards. The success of this plan had far reaching effects on all of the aviation units in-theatre, for it freed up major bases such as Suwon, Seoul City and Kimpo.

This meant that most, if not all, of the fighter squadrons that had been flying long missions from bases in Japan could now find a home on South Korean soil, thus cutting their flying time in half. The 8th FG's two Mustang squadrons were among those brought forward, and on 25 September the 811th Engineer Aviation Battalion (EAB) arrived from Guam in preparation of this move. Their job was to rapidly refurbish the 'beat-up' airfields at Kimpo and Suwon.

Capt Francis B Clark flew with the 35th FBS during this period, seeing action in both the F-80 and F-51 from bases in Japan and Korea;

'One day we flew several missions in F-80s over Korea out of our base at Itazuke. We recovered at Tsuiki AB (Code named 'Sun Valley') late in the evening, and then flew pre-dawn strikes the next morning in the F-51. I can recall flying at least five Mustang sorties in one day out of Suwon. We were close to a retreating North Korean army, and the missions were short in duration.'

As Capt Clark noted, the 35th and 36th FBSs had been flying their combat sorties out of Tsuiki AB. At the time, there was no room for them to set up at Taegu (K-2) or Pohang (K-3), although the capture of Suwon (K-13) created the possibility of at least one of the squadrons setting up in-theatre. However, since the base was in such poor condition, and its PSP (pierced-steel planking) proved to be more of a liability than an asset, the units stayed in Japan until the 811th EAB had whipped Suwon into an acceptable shape. On 7 October the 35th FBS was finally able to fly in, leaving the 36th to continue those long over-water missions alone.

Overall control of Suwon was passed to the 51st FIW who, at last, had the opportunity to get their F-80s into Korea, and stretch their sorties along the Yalu so as to include some precious loiter time on patrol. The allocation of the base to the F-80 wing placed the 35th FIS in a bind, because there was only enough space on the airfield for three squadrons of Shooting Stars. The much needed break came on 30 October when Kimpo was also opened 'for business'. The 35th immediately moved up from Suwon, and the 36th followed suit by bringing all of their equipment over from Japan. With both squadrons finally in-theatre, the 8th FG was able to 'lash out' against the enemy with much more destructive force.

CHINESE INVASION

Just as the UN forces were nearing the banks of the Yalu River, and it seemed certain that the war would be over by Christmas, the Chinese entered the war. This left friendly ground forces staring at 100,000 fresh enemy troops across the battlefield. Retreat was the only recourse, and on 26 November 1950, all hell broke loose

BELOW *The ordnance crews from the various Mustang squadrons gathered up anything they could find to use against the enemy forces. This 35th FBS fighter-bomber has been loaded with two huge 'Tiny Tim' rockets that were obtained from a nearby Marine Corsair squadron! These missiles were slightly erratic when fired, but when they impacted a target the blow was invariably fatal. This shot was taken at a damp Kimpo AB in the autumn of 1950 (Francis Clark)*

ABOVE RIGHT *Capt Joe 'Whistling Joe' Rogers settles in the cockpit of his 36th FBS Mustang at the start of yet another mission over the frontline. Rogers obtained his nickname by attaching a series of hollow tubes to the underside of his F-51. When he started a steep bomb run, the air going through the tubes would make a high-pitched screeching sound that caused the enemy troops to break cover and stick their heads out of the trenches to see what was making the noise (William O'Donnell)*

LEFT *A young armourer from the 36th FBS diligently loads 0.50-cal ammo belts into 'his' Mustang. This weapon, along with napalm, proved to be the most effective against NKPA troops. When the Chinese entered the conflict towards the end of 1950, most of their casualties were caused by napalm, which was also dropped by F-80s and F-82s (William O'Donnell)*

ABOVE *FAC with the RoKA's 1st Division was hazardous duty. This photo was taken by Lt Col Bill O'Donnell whilst working with the 1st close to Seoul. On the road below this elevated position, a raging tank battle was being slugged out. By the time this shot was taken, the fighter-bombers were already on their way to help out (William O'Donnell)*

when Chinese Gen Lin Piao 'sprang the trap' against the American Eighth Army.

In the weeks immediately prior to the Chinese offensive, Mustang pilots that were flying interdiction missions along the Yalu reported seeing fast, swept-wing, all-silver jets over the Antung area. USAF Intelligence did not place much stock in these reports, as the MiG-15 was still very little known in the West.

It did not take long for the MiG pilots to muster up the courage to attack the slower moving Mustangs, however, with one of the first squadrons to encounter the new jet fighter being the 35th FBS. According to unit commander, Capt Ray Lancaster, MiG encounters began on 7 November when a flight of F-51s was jumped.

Flight lead on this mission was Lt Harris Boyce, who noticed a pair of MiG-15s above them at 30,000 ft as he was patrolling over the Yalu at 12,000 ft. The jets first passed overhead, before diving straight down at the F-51s. In response to this attack, the flight broke hard right, with Boyce pulling a fast 180° turn that put him on the tail of the trailing MiG. Making full use of this split-second advantage, Boyce fired off a long burst, and noticed

numerous hits all over the MiG's fuselage. The communist fighter then seemed to briefly go out of control as it headed north, but no explosion or fire was seen, so Boyce had to settle for a 'probable'. Capt Lancaster recalls further details;

'Early the next morning after Boyce's encounter, I led a flight of four Mustangs back to the same area. We watched 11 MiG-15s take off from Antung airfield. In a few seconds, one of our flight called out "Bogies at eight o'clock high". We were positioned at 10,000 ft when the call came. I initiated a slow turn into them as they came down at us. We were facing them head on, and I remember their speed being so much greater than ours. We had little chance to get in firing positions. However, I rolled out on the last MiG as he came through us, and holding the trigger down, I poured 365 rounds of .50 calibre fire toward a rapidly disappearing silver streak! It had happened so fast, and fortunately none of us were hit. I'm sure none of the MiGs were hit either. They did not come back at us, and we returned safely to base.'

This was an indicator of what lay ahead for the F-51 pilots when they ventured too close to the Yalu!

LEFT *The march to the Yalu had begun, and the shifting front made Mustang missions longer in duration. Although the conditions at Suwon were rough, everybody had a 'warm feeling', even with the cold weather setting in, as it looked like the war would be over by Christmas. Seen at the extreme left of this group of 36th FBS pilots is the 8th FBG's CO, Lt Col William T Samways (William O'Donnell)*

BELOW *UN Intelligence indicated that the North Koreans had set up a command post in specific area of this village, so F-51s from the 35th FBS were called in to hit the target with napalm. The results of the strike were recorded by a Mustang pilot, who took this shot in September 1950 (Al Wimer)*

RIGHT *Five 36th FBS pilots pose at Suwon as they rest between missions 'up north'. Second from right is Lt Robert Fogg, who came over on the Boxer with the group of volunteer Mustang pilots in mid-July 1950. A short time after this photo was taken, the squadron moved their operations up to the North Korean capital, Pyongyang (William O'Donnell)*

ABOVE RIGHT *During the early autumn of 1950, the success of the Inchon landings forced the Mustangs to fly missions all the way up to the Manchurian border, despite still being based 'way down south'. This photo shows 'Contour William' flight, from the 35th FBS, heading north with a full load of rockets and napalm. The shot was taken from the left 'slot' in the formation (Roy Bell)*

As the UN forces had pushed north towards the Chinese border, so the missions for the Fifth AF aircraft in-theatre became lengthy affairs once again. However, following the Chinese invasion things rapidly changed. What lay ahead for the units were some of the shortest and fastest base moves that any squadron made during the war.

Right after the 35th and 36th FBSs had set up operations out of Kimpo, they were notified that they could move all the way north to Pyongyang. On 25 November the units pushed forward, with all of their ground equipment going by train. The bitter cold winter weather had already started to set in, and the new base was well within range of NKPAF 'heckler' Po-2 biplanes. The new base was hit three times by these slow, nocturnal, nuisance raiders, the first of these strikes taking place on 28 November when a lone Po-2 hit the base at 0300 hours with several fragmentation bombs. They hit the aircraft dispersal area and 11 Mustangs were damaged – three of these so badly that they could not be repaired prior to the base being hastily evacuated in the face of a rapidly approaching Chinese Army.

Five days later it was time to 'bug out' again! At this point in time, all three Mustang wings were operating north of the 38th Parallel.

With the communists just miles away when the evacuation order was given, there was no time to pack equipment, load it onto railcars and move it south. The commanding officer of the 36th FBS, Lt Col William O'Donnell, relates the details of those last days at Pyongyang, and also the fate of his colourful Mustang, *'Mac's Revenge'* (44-84974);

'A day or so before we "bugged out", Lt Paul Carlisle flew a mission in my assigned F-51. On a low-level strafing pass, he hit some power lines and they wrapped all around the aircraft. He couldn't get out, so he nursed the aircraft back to Pyongyang and bellied in. With our orders to pull out, there was no time to repair the aircraft or get it back to flying condition.

'Here we were with our equipment still loaded on rail cars, yet there was no time to get them out of there. The last man to leave Pyongyang was the group commander, Col Jack Price. He had a C-47, I think, and his crew chief was with him, and kept the engines running, while Col Price made the rounds, setting fire to anything that could be of value to the Chinese. He rode up on the wing of my damaged *'Mac's Revenge'* in his jeep, got out and poured gasoline all over the Mustang and threw a lit Zippo lighter into the cockpit. That was the last of my F-51! As Price climbed into his C-47, the Chinese were pouring over the end of the runway. He lifted off and made it safely back to Seoul City Airport . The next day, we launched several of our Mustangs to destroy the rail cars that held all of our equipment up at Pyongyang.'

1Lt Peter W Richardson was involved in the mission that had seen *'Mac's Revenge'* so badly damaged, being

LEFT By late August 1950 the 35th FBS had received their full complement of Mustangs. The missions were long and overwater, and although the Inchon landings were only a few weeks away, until the Pusan Perimeter had been broken out of, these Mustangs would have to operate from Tsuiki AB, in Japan, as shown here (Roy Bell)

RIGHT *The badly damaged North Korean airbases captured in the wake of Inchon had a sinister look to them. The conditions encountered by the crews were a notch below what they were used to at Taegu and Pohang, as this view of a hangar at Yonpo airfield (K-27) clearly shows. One of two major airbases used by the NKPAF, Yonpo was located on the east coast, south of Hungnam. This bombed out hangar was used by the ordnance squadron, whilst the dismembered F-51 hulk in the background probably belonged to the 39th FIS (Phillip DeLong)*

BELOW RIGHT *The 35th FBS traded in their F-80Cs for a full complement of Mustangs that had come over aboard the Boxer. One such aircraft was 47-5002, which had clearly been assigned to the Indiana ANG prior to receiving the call to active duty (Paul Carlsen)*

one of four pilots enticed into an elaborate trap that had been set by the North Koreans at the intersection of two roads. He was flying in the number two slot, with Lt Carlisle in the lead, as he relates;

'We were on an armed reconnaissance mission with a flight of four Mustangs from the 36th FBS. We spotted a truck sitting out in the open where two roads crossed. Lead went right in after it, and as he finished strafing he started to pull up. Suddenly, there was a small explosion on the ground, and this twisting mass of cable went straight up in the air, completely engulfing lead's Mustang! It wrapped under his engine nacelle and over both wings, then looped around his aft fuselage and trailed at least 100 ft behind, forming a 40° to 60° cone.

'Lt Carlisle was placed under a tremendous physical strain to keep his F-51 airborne and level. Once we had cleared the area, there was an idea tossed around amongst us pilots that maybe I could come up behind him and cut the cable. That idea was quickly discarded, however, as it would probably have resulted in my aircraft getting entangled also, and both of us would have gone down. Carlisle, through his piloting skills, was able to nurse the aircraft back to our base at Pyongyang.

'His engine power was on high RPMs, while slowly descending. As he came in low and cleared the Taedong River, the trailing cable was slapping the water. Reaching the edge of the runway at about 150 mph, Carlisle bellied the fighter in across the airfield and into the neighbouring rice paddies. I believe that he was injured during the landing, but was pulled safely out.'

Thus was the fate of the CO's favourite Mustang!

SEARCH AND RESCUE

The art of Search and Rescue (SAR) was in its infancy during the Korean War, and it would not effectively mature until the long and futile war in Vietnam some 15 years later. Nonetheless, helicopters were occasionally pulling off some spectacular extractions deep behind enemy lines. One of the first such SAR missions to be successfully completed was flown on Thanksgiving Day – 25 November – 1950, and involved the 36th FBS. Lt Robert S Fogg recalls the details;

'We had an eight-ship mission up, which bombed the runway at Kangye. We each carried two 500-lb GPs, two 150-gal drop tanks and 1800 rounds of 0.50-cal ammo. We pre-briefed on a high altitude release of the bombs due to known AA around the base. I was in Blue Flight, with Harold Kinison as my wingman. I was in the last echelon, so I was able to observe the hits on the runway, and also the flak that was all around us. Kinison called out that he had been hit, and by the time I pulled up alongside him, his aircraft was smoking and the prop was windmilling. He had no choice but to jump. We followed

RIGHT *The 35th FBS's Lt Roy Bell and Leon Pagan pose by Lt Bob Dewald's RAMBLIN' RECK III at a forward base in South Korea. Bell would move over to the 18th FBW when the 35th reverted back to the F-80 (Roy Bell)*

his 'chute as it went into a wooded area.

'Blue Flight circled until we were low on fuel, at which point we headed home. The next morning, our CO, Bill O'Donnell, went to Fifth AF HQ and requested a rescue effort, but was turned down. The reason given was that the air force didn't have any helicopters in the area. This didn't stop us, however! We headed for a small strip that was being used by the Army for their L-5s and a few helicopters. We explained the situation to them, but they were a little hesitant due to the great distance into enemy territory that had to be flown – they explained that their fuel would not hold out for the time they would be airborne.

'However, we worked out a solution by rigging the "chopper" up to carry jerrycans of fuel inside so that it could refuel itself in flight. We provided the escort in our Mustangs. About ten miles south of where Kinison bailed out, we flew ahead in the hope of locating him, but had no luck! As the "chopper" approached, we moved on to the south, and about five miles from where he should have been, we spotted a flare fired out of the wooded area.

'As the helo started to move in closer, he reported that he was taking small arms fire, and would have to leave the area! About that time, Kinison darted out of the trees and the "chopper" pilot dropped down low enough for him to grab the right wheel, and the crewman hauled him in. With the groundfire getting ever closer, we moved out of the area quickly. It was truly Thanksgiving Day! The

next day we visited Kinison in the hospital, and he told us of his two days spent evading troops and tanks. He stated that the tanks were hidden inside the houses, and we later confirmed that information and destroyed the houses. When he was strong enough to leave the hospital, Kinison requested a secret intelligence briefing with Fifth AF HQ. At that point he revealed that the enemy he had been evading were indeed Chinese troops, and not NKPA. This was one of the first indications that the Chinese had entered the war!'

The two squadrons of the 8th FBG would be the first to be ordered to give up the Mustang, their tenure with the veteran fighter being the shortest of the six units that were hurriedly outfitted during the early days of the war. The pull out from Pyongyang was completed on 3 December, the units' moving south to Seoul City Airport (K-16). This major staging base was located on the south side of the Han River within sight of South Korea's capital city.

Just five days after leaving Pyongyang, the 35th and 36th FBSs were again on the move – this time to Itazuke AB to begin their transition back onto the F-80. The 8th FBG's 80th FBS, which had retained its Shooting Stars throughout, and had been attached to the 51st FIW at Suwon, now also returned into the fold once again. The 'Fighting 8th' was once more intact.

With the removal of the 35th and 36th FBSs, just four frontline USAF fighter squadrons now remained operational with an ever-dwindling number of war-weary Mustangs.

Chapter Four

18th FIGHTER BOMBER GROUP

At one point during the first few months of the war, there were four wings operating F-51s in-theatre. However, as the attrition rate grew and the number of Mustangs diminished, so did the squadrons flying them. Indeed, things got so bad that the 8th and 35th FBGs eventually turned over their World War 2-era fighters to the 18th FBG and transitioned back onto the F-80C. Aside from the latter group, the 67th Tactical Reconnaissance Wing (TRW) also continued to use the F/RF-51 in the photo role until late in the war.

When looking at the war as a whole, it was the 18th FBG that is always identified with the mighty Mustang in Korea. To the media, Fifth AF and South Korean President Syngman Rhee, they were known as the 'Truckbusters',

but to the personnel within the group itself, they were the 'Dogpatch Gang'. The 18th FBG took an ageing, highly vulnerable, World War 2 fighter and effectively rewrote the history books. All of the pilots that flew the F-51 in combat did so at great personal risk to themselves, for they were waging war using machines that were never designed for the close support and interdiction roles.

When the Korean War started, the battle seasoned 18th FBW was operating out of Clark AB, in the Philippines. The wing was comprised of three squadrons, namely the 12th, 44th and 67th FBSs, all of which were flying the new F-80C. The USAF's all-jet force in the Philippines was staffed with an abundance of veteran combat pilots that could more than 'hold their own' with

BELOW *During the spring and summer months of 1951, Seoul City Airport (K-16) was a major staging area for several squadrons of Fifth AF fighter-bombers. Viewed through the props of this Mustang is a line-up of 12th FBS 'Foxy Few' F-51Ds, as well as a Navy AD Skyraider and F4U Corsair. With the exception of newly-arrived replacement aircraft, 12th FBS Mustangs always wore a trademark red sharksmouth (Tom Shockley)*

RIGHT *This is where the 18th FBG legend began – Pusan AB South Korea (K-9). The conditions were so crude that many commented that it looked like 'Dogpatch', which was a popular comic strip in the US. Coupled with the fact it was officially designated K-9 (Canine), the reference stuck. A few weeks later the group was adopted by cartoonist Al Capp, who designed unique emblems for all of the units within the 18th FBG (Lee Gomes)*

FAR RIGHT *During the early days of the war, the frontline was so close to the Mustangs' operating bases that each aircraft usually flew several sorties in one day. The key to achieving this phenomenal feat rested with the armourers and maintenance people, who had the ability to quickly turn these ageing fighters around between flights. This picture shows a 12th FBS 'Foxy Few' Mustang being reloaded with 0.50 cal ammo in preparation for its next foray over enemy lines (Ed Nebinger)*

the best of them. When the 'battle flag was run up the pole', it was the 12th FBS that was chosen to furnish the pilots to man the interim 'Dallas' Squadron, which had been formed to fly the F-51 in Korea. This unit was commanded by Maj Harry Moreland.

Although the 'Dallas' Squadron was also manned by pilots pulled from other units within the Thirteenth AF, it consisted mostly of men from the 12th FBS. The unit was activated on 3 July. Exactly a week later the Fifth AF was also ordered to form up a provisional fighter squadron to fly the F-51s too – this would be known as the 51st FS(P). The unit subsequently took command of the 'Bout One' and 'Dallas' units once in-theatre, commencing operations from Taegu AB on 15 July.

Two days prior to this, Gen Timberlake obtained permission to move the 18th FBG (essentially, just the 67th FBS) from the Philippines to Japan. The group duly came north-east on 30 July, then pressed on to Taegu on 4 August. In the meantime, the 18th FBW remained back at Clark AB. At this time, the newly-formed 51st FS(P) reverted back to its original designation of the 12th FBS. Now committed in group strength to the war, the 18th FBG desperately needed all of its backup and support units (left behind at Clark), so on 8 August the 6002nd Tactical Support Wing (TSW) was formed. The new wing was not replaced by the 18th FBW until 2 December 1950.

One of the immediate problems facing the fighter-bomber units in Korea was differentiating between the enemy on the ground, and the tens of thousands of refugees that were flooding south in an effort to escape the NKPA. Their numbers were so great that the invaders easily caught them up and used them for protection by mingling in with the massive crowds. Maj Harry Moreland recalls one of these early missions out of Taegu that saw him and his wingman, Capt 'Chappie' James, trying to seek out the enemy in the confusion below them;

'We were on the verge of having to pull out of our base at Taegu and move back to Japan. We were flying as many missions as possible in order to slow the enemy's advance. We were in touch with a FAC who told us he had spotted a large number of enemy troops coming down the road on foot. When we dropped down low, we noticed that they were mostly women and children, so we opted not to attack. Instead, we flew up a valley and located a number of camouflaged vehicles.

'The North Koreans had dug holes in the hillside, run the trucks into the hole, and then covered them with branches. Some of the branches were a little off-colour, so it was easy for us to spot the target. Also, invariably there were tyre tracks leading to the holes. So instead of strafing some very questionable civilian types on the road, we destroyed about 20 vehicles – some of which were loaded with ammunition, as evidenced by the explosions. Both "Chappie" and I were very pleased at the option we had chosen.'

After a very brief return to Ashiya by the 12th, it

BELOW *Capt Howard I Price of the 67th FBS poses by his fully-loaded Mustang prior to flying another mission against the NKPA tank columns. Note the shaped charges on the rockets, which were highly explosive and used mostly against enemy armour. Capt Price successfully tangled with North Korean Yak-9s on 3 August and 6 November 1950, being credited with 1.5 aerial victories and a solitary ground kill (H I Price)*

LEFT *At one time there were eight squadrons of Mustangs flying in Korea (this included the 'Aussies' and South Africans). On just about every sortie, their Mustangs were loaded with rockets, and in order to keep up with the demand, an assembly line technique was set up to prepare the rounds for fitment to the F-51s. This view shows the 'line' at Pusan (K-9), and a local peasant boy, in the late summer of 1950 (C E Trumbo)*

ABOVE *The consumption rate of belt 0.50-cal machine gun ammo even exceeded the demand for rockets! The demand proved to be so great that the support wings had ordnance crews assigned that did nothing but reload the guns. Here, Capt Howard I Price of the 67th FBS talks with one of the armorers in the squadron prior to the latter reloading the Mustang in the background during the late summer of 1950 (Charles Schreffler)*

joined the 67th FBS at Pusan to fly defence missions over the ever-shrinking Pusan Perimeter. The battered UN forces on the ground were now struggling to blunt the attacks of a vastly superior NKPA, which boasted not only greater manpower, but also more tanks, howitzers and trucks. Although the defence of Pusan proved to be a classic 'holding action', it surely did not come out of any military text book. Indeed, by mid-August the only thing keeping the North Koreans from consuming the peninsula was the USAF and its fighter-bombers, each of which usually flew multiple sorties every day.

Capt Duane 'Bud' Biteman kept the figures for the 12th FBS as the unit's S-2 officer – statistics that would have looked impressive in any war. The unit's efforts were even more outstanding when one takes into account the conditions in which it had to operate at Taegu and Pusan. His figures, set out below, clearly show what the squadron achieved between 15 July and 31 August 1950. In that time the 12th FBS (which could boast just 20 Mustangs) flew some 2650 hours and averaged 33 sorties sorties per day. Biteman's final tally on sorties flown was set at 1438 – all by the 12th!

	Destroyed	Probables	Damaged
Tanks	63	24	108
Armoured Vehicles	15	1	14
Trucks	263	10	212
Misc. Vehicles	225	24	218
Locomotives	25	2	31
Boxcars	78	10	212
Boats	37	2	42
Artillery Pieces	49	8	38
Fuel Dumps	40	0	0
Warehouses	69	4	61
Bridges	7	0	32
Carts	34	0	18
Dams	0	0	2
Tunnels	0	0	11
Aircraft Ground	3	0	9
Aircraft Air	1	0	0

During this period, the 12th FBS fired 8500 rockets, dropped 2300 bombs and fired 860,000 rounds of 0.50-cal. The squadron in turn suffered the loss of four pilots killed, with a further three wounded. It also lost six Mustangs.

LEFT *Capt Jerry Hogue, one of the more experienced Mustang pilots in the 12th Fighter Squadron (FS) relaxes by his F-51 after a mission. Note his World War 2 type leather helmet. This photograph was taken in early 1951 whilst the United Nations' forces were trying to stabilise the frontlines in the wake of China's entry into the war (Roy Bell)*

RIGHT *The 67th FBS's CO, Capt Arnold 'Moon' Mullins (left), chats with one of his pilots, Capt H I Price – note the victory notches cut into the pole in front of the squadron operations tent. This shot was taken on 6 November 1950, right after Price had been given credit for his 1.5 kills. Between the two of them, both pilots had destroyed 5.5 enemy aircraft (this included air and ground kills) by war's end (H I Price)*

FAR RIGHT *Two of the original pilots that saw action during the very early days with the 'Dallas' Squadron take time out to have their picture taken with some of their sharksmouth Mustangs in the background. On the left is Capt Frank C Buzze and to the right Maj Harry Moreland, who was commanding officer of the 12th FBS at the time. This photo was taken at Pusan during the dark days of the shrinking Pusan Perimeter. It was during this time that the 'Dogpatch' legend originated (Harry Moreland)*

As can be seen from these statistics, the 12th FBS clearly had more targets than it could handle. The NKPA did not seem to mind that its men and equipment were out in the open during the day, as long as they were moving in one direction – south! Maj Harry Moreland recalls a typical sortie that he flew on a hot August day;

'This mission was comprised of two F-51s flying out of Taegu AB (K-2). We were on an interdiction sortie that covered everything between Seoul and Taejon. We had strafed a few targets and had caught a couple of trucks out in the open with our napalm. Satisfied that nothing else was running the road, we headed back to base.

'As we were cruising back at a relatively low altitude, I noticed a huge haystack in the middle of a field which had large tread marks leading right up to it. I circled around and came across to get a better look. No doubt about it – there was a tank hidden under the straw! We had already expended out napalm load, so all we had were 0.50-cal rounds, which posed little threat to a tank. Anyhow, we made a few passes over the tank, spraying lead all over the haystack.

BELOW *This F-51 must have hit a tree or telephone pole on one of its low level runs, judging by the isolated nature of the damage inflicted to the wing leading edge. The undercarriage door to the left of the photo also appears to have suffered in the impact. The Mustangs, although very vulnerable to small arms fire, often worked at treetop level during their missions. The squadron operating this aircraft remains unidentified (C E Trumbo)*

'In a few minutes, we noticed that the hay was on fire. This brought about another good idea. Why not buzz right over the haystack and fan the flames? We did it and it worked. The flames were engulfing everything in that stack. Moments later, there was a large explosion and the tank blew up. That was one T-34 that would not be back in operation.'

Since the Mustang squadrons were the first units to inhabit the airfields on Korean soil, they enjoyed the least stability of any USAF assets committed to the war. Indeed, the first few weeks of the war saw the UN forces almost 'booted off' the peninsula, and it was only when the Marines stormed ashore at Inchon that the NKPA was finally stopped in its tracks. What followed was a series of see-saw movements for the F-51 squadrons as UN forces firstly pushed north towards the Yalu, then hurriedly retreated back south in the face of the invading Chinese Army.

Once the frontline began to stabilise at about the 38th parallel in early 1951, Mustang bases became a little more permanent. By this time, the attrition rate inflicted on the F-51 population had taken a heavy toll, and gradually those squadrons that had given up jets in the early months of the war began to turn over their surviving Mustangs to the 18th FBG. Gone were the 8th and 35th FBGs, and the RAAF's No 77 Sqn replaced its Mustangs with new Meteor F 8s in April.

The two 18th FBG squadrons that had been involved in the conflict almost from the very start had quickly learned to live virtually out of a footlocker and tool box. A quick look at the 12th FBS's movement records clearly shows why – Taegu AB on 28 July, Ashiya AB on 8 August, Pusan AB on 8 September, Pyongyang on 20 November, Suwon on 3 December and Chinhae on 22 December. The 67th FBS followed an almost identical pattern, with the exception that they were occasionally either a few days behind or ahead of the 12th on some of the moves – Taegu AB on 28 July, Ashiya AB on 8 August, Pusan AB on 8 September, Pyongyang on 27 November, Suwon AB on 1 December and finally Chinhae AB on 9 December.

The final airfield in both movement records was the old Japanese seaplane base at Chinhae (K-10), which had been taken over in December by the newly-arrived 18th FBW. The wing would remain at this airfield until the final months of the war, when all three units finally converted to the F-86F.

SHOOT DOWNS

The number of Mustang pilots that were shot down flying over Korea formed a large fraternity by the time the aircraft was finally replaced by the Sabre. Maj Moreland was one of those individuals to have his aircraft shot out from beneath him by groundfire. As with most Mustangs

LEFT *Lt MacCauley, who flew with the 18th FBW, had his photo taken at the bomb dump at Hoengsong (K-46) during a visit to the base. He is sitting on a 1000-lb GP, whilst those lined up in the next row are 500-lb GPs. On a typical day's flying for the wing, all of the bombs visible in this view would easily be used (Bruce Clark)*

downed by the North Koreans, the major's aircraft had its liquid-cooled Merlin engine starved of coolant when it suffered flak damage. The powerplant quickly overheated, forcing Moreland to belly in short of his base at Taegu;

'Frank Buzze and I were strafing targets in the Taejon area when I took some rounds in the coolant system. I immediately started climbing for altitude. The mixture control was placed in "full rich", allowing the engine to run as cool as possible, and hopefully allow me to make it back to friendly territory. At about 3000 ft I started to lose power, which eliminated any possibility of gaining altitude. I commenced a very gradual descent toward our base. At this time, the frontline was centred around the Naktong River, and all I wanted to do was cross it and belly in.

'At the rate I was dropping, there would be no way to clear the river. Instead, I would land right in the middle of it. Recalling the Pilot' Handbook, I instantly remembered the passage which told you not to ditch a P-51 because it would break in half at the cockpit. It also stated that if you could not avoid a water crash-landing, drop a wing into the water before you came into full contact with it. I followed this procedure, and when the wing hit the water, it caused the plane to veer sharply and hit the water almost broadside! I was able to exit the aircraft bruised, but intact.

'I made it safely to a sandbar on the east bank, where I was suddenly surrounded by about 500 Koreans in white clothing. I didn't know if they were friendly or not. Now, I' m not a smoker, but I did remember that I had a pack of Lucky Strikes in my flying suit. I took the pack out and held them over my head. Seconds later, I was engulfed by this sea of white. Buzze thought I was being attacked and almost strafed us. I passed the pack around, and it was like sitting down and smoking an Indian peacepipe! Before the vehicle showed up to get me, the Koreans formed a line, and as they passed by me, they touched me and said "thank-you" in Korean. It was a very

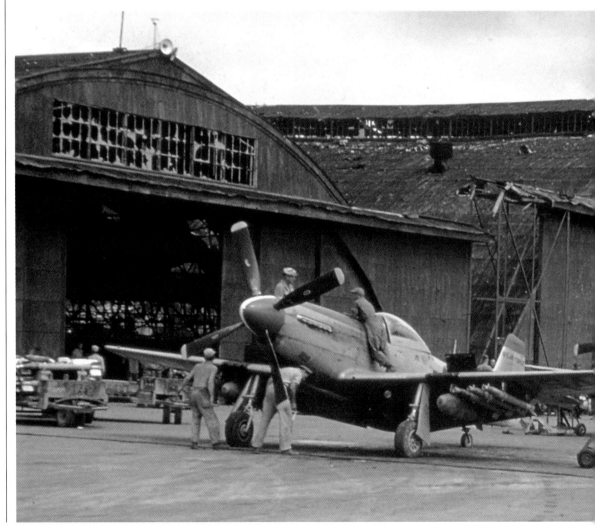

RIGHT *When the 35th FBG pulled its 40th FBS back to Japan in early 1951, its 39th FIS joined the 18th FBW, as did all its surviving Mustangs. This photo shows a quartet of ex-35th FBG blue-blinkered nose aircraft lined up for rearming between sorties at the 18th FBW's major staging base at Seoul City (K-16). The photo was taken on 16 July 1951 (Walt Burke)*

LEFT *The most effective weapon that was delivered by the Mustang squadrons during the Korean War was napalm, and any NKPA or Chinese Army PoW would tell you that it was feared by every man in their outfit. It took preparation, and an assembly line technique like that adopted for the unguided rockets, to get enough napalm ready to satisfy the 18th TFW's daily rate of consumption (Max Tomich)*

LEFT *From 15 July until 31 August 1950, the 12th FBS fired 8500 rockets and dropped over 2500 tanks of napalm. Broken down, this meant that the unit was expending 60 of these tanks (seen here being filled by both USAF and Korean personnel) per day (Steven Levandoski)*

unusual ending to a truly bizarre mission!'

Before the Pusan Perimeter was broken and the fighting shifted north, the 12th and 67th FBSs were forced to keep their fighters in the air while operating out of a very crowded Pusan AB. The latter airfield, along with Pohang, were the two southernmost bases on the peninsula, and both sites were finding it increasingly difficult to sustain heavy fighter-bomber traffic in amongst a constant stream of large transport aircraft that were lined up on the ground waiting to unload vital supplies. The never ending procession of USAF transports alone was 'beating the hell' out of both airfields.

The constant struggle to find take-off and recovery slots for fully-loaded Mustangs operating from rough forward bases like Pusan or Pohang further fuelled the anxiety levels of the pilots and mission planners of the 12th and 67th FBSs. Things got so bad at these airfields that for a while it was difficult to tell what worried pilots more – getting shot up on the mission, or knowing that they were in for a rough landing, sometimes with heavy battle damage, upon their return to base. For some individuals, the easiest part of the mission was firing the guns and dropping the bombs!

Despite the Mustang's vulnerability to ground fire, and the increasing proliferation of NKPA targets, pilots continued to press home their attacks. On a mission flown on 1 September 1950 by Maj James Peek and Lt Ted Baader of the 12th FS's 'Foxy Few Gang', the latter pilot destroyed several targets, but on each firing pass his fighter absorbed numerous hits from heavy ground fire. Maj Peek recalls the sortie;

'Our objective for the mission was to fly close air support. We launched from Ashiya AB, in Japan, and upon reaching our assigned area, we checked in with a FAC in the Hyopchon area. We were given several good targets, and as I was flying high cover, I saw Lt Baader score two direct hits on an enemy self-propelled vehicle. We then moved on over to the west around Hill No 409. The visibility in this area was hazy due to all the smoke from previous strikes, and we were also fully aware that the terrain below us was dangerously mountainous.

'We were taking turns making passes over enemy troop positions when, on the third pass, I noticed Baader's Mustang momentarily go out of control, but then quickly right itself. He immediately got into position for another pass, and this time he seemed to take even more hits from ground fire. His aircraft then seemed to briefly lose directional control, before he righted it and continued to

LEFT *A few of the pilots that were involved in the early 12th FBS operations out of Pusan take turns in riding their 'liberated' North Korean motorcycle-sidecar combination around the base. Recreation facilities were non-existent at any base in South Korea during the early part of the war (Lee Gomes)*

BELOW *Two seasoned combat pilots from the 39th FIS relax by NOHEROHERE at the 18th FBW's forward staging base at Hoengsong (K-46). On the left is Maj Jack Davis, commanding officer of the squadron, and to the right Capt 'Rocky' Brett, who was assigned to this F-51D. Brett went on to achieve the rank of lieutenant general in the USAF prior to retirement (Devol 'Rocky' Brett)*

make two more extremely low firing passes.

'With our ordnance expended, and Baader's Mustang damaged, we were forced to land at Taegu, which was the closest airfield. In spite of the heavy battle damage inflicted on Baader's F-51, he succeeded in making a normal landing. The FAC later confirmed that by pressing home his attacks, Baader had succeeded in killing or wounding over 100 enemy troops.'

WINTER WEATHER

The winter set in early in 1950, and by November it was bitterly cold in the northern extremities of the peninsula. Maj Moreland remembers one of those days when his unit was 'running the roads' north of Pyongyang, searching for targets;

'It was late November, and the weather was so cold that the water in our canteens froze solid in our tents! The war looked like it would soon be over, however. This day we were in a four-ship, spread out over a major highway running up toward Manchuria. Suddenly, we received a frantic call from a "Mosquito" (FAC) pilot who told us that he could use all the help he could get. When we found him we could see an endless number of American vehicles stacked up in full retreat from the oncoming Chinese Army. They were taking intense fire from both sides of the road, and several trucks were burning. Blocking the column was a friendly tank that had been disabled.

'We began dropping our napalm along the ridges overlooking the column. When these were gone, we ran out the "full nine yards" of 0.50-cal ammo. As we used up everything, we called out to other Mustangs in the area and they began arriving. We stayed around long enough to see the division have the time to push the tank out of the way and get the column moving. We had given them the "safe" time they needed to get the road unblocked.

'There is no way of knowing how many Chinese we took out on those ridges. I never cheered so loud in my life as I did when I saw that column start moving again! As we flew back to our base, we radioed ahead for more aircraft to be sent up to help the column keep moving south. They made it OK, but took heavy casualties. Our FAC on the ground with the troops was Capt Mal Edens. He did not make it out.'

The war in Korea spanned 37 long months. It appeared for a short while that the month of September 1950 would have the most impact on the war, with the Inchon landings, followed by the UN forces breaking out of the Pusan Perimeter. But it was easily overshadowed by the month of November, when the Chinese Army stormed south across the border into Korea.

As previously mentioned, one of the immediate results of the Chinese intervention was the appearance

RIGHT *The influence of cartoonist Al Capp was found all over the 18th's base at Chinhae (K-10), which developed a personality all its own as it grew in size. Note the various and sundry uniforms shown in this photo, reflecting that the USAF was definitely going through a transitional period from World War 2 to the Cold War era (George Bach)*

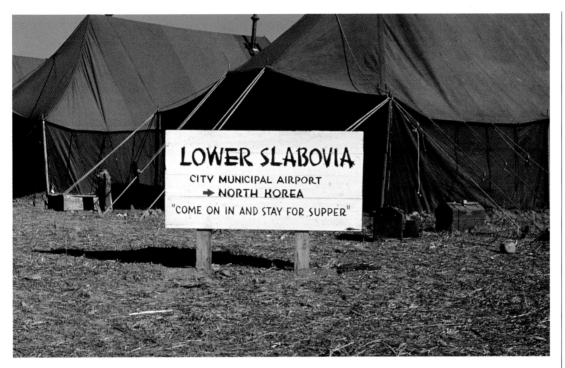

of the MiG-15. This triggered the eventual appearance in-theatre of the latest aircraft from the United States' arsenal, the F-86 Sabre. Both jets would be locked in mortal combat for aerial supremacy for the remainder of the war, and the escalation of the conflict effectively 'kick-started' an arms race between the Soviet Union and the Free World that would last into the late 1980s. In the short term, Korea would become the testing ground for the next generation of weapons.

The Chinese invasion had seen the war's centre of gravity shift abruptly to the most north-westerly region of North Korea. Huge numbers of troops, supported by tanks, artillery and trucks, were literally flooding through the 'gates' of Manchuria in a southerly direction. All bomber and fighter-bomber efforts were quickly focused on the area that would soon become known as 'MiG Alley'. The communist fighters that proliferated in this area came from airfields known as Antung and Mukden, where MiG-15s could be found in abundance. The jet menace was not the only aerial threat waiting to pounce on an unwary flight of Mustangs, however, for the NKPAF still possessed enough piston-engined Yak fighters to occasionally 'spice up' operations at medium to low altitudes as well.

Capt Robert Thresher of the 67th FBS recalls just such an encounter which took place on 1 November 1950. It happened while all of the members of his flight were concentrating on their ground targets;

'Our objective was to work with a "Mosquito" pilot, and our first target was to bust up a roadblock. We made some passes and opened it up. As my wingman, Capt A R 'Dad' Flake, and I moved further north, I commented that it was unusual that we had not encountered any ground fire. All of a sudden these big orange balls were snapping across my left wing, and I yelled "Flak"! Just as I got that out, a blur whizzed by me, and at that instant I realised that my problem wasn't ground fire, but a real fast Yak fighter!

'I immediately initiated evasive action by taking a hard left turn in the hope of hooking up with my wingman, but alas he was on the tail of another Yak. My bogey had disappeared, and I knew he was up there in the sun, but didn't know where. Suddenly, the "Mosquito" pilot yelled, "He's on your tail!" I turned my head in time to catch the winking of the Yak's 12.7 mm machine guns and his 20 mm cannon. I went into a sharp turn and the blood drained out of my head, causing me to witness a "grey out".

'In my panic, I knew the Yak could turn inside of me, but I held the stick over. Rolling out, I observed that the enemy pilot had gone across the top of my Mustang, and taking advantage of his speed, he had pulled into a tight loop Now he was above me and that put him in a good position! I swung hard left to pass directly beneath him and to keep him from coming out of the loop right on my tail! He was watching me, and he must have held his stick back too long, because he stalled out. He spun all the way down from 6000 ft.

'The Yak pilot recovered, and for a split-second I thought I would tighten my turn and jump him while he

FAR LEFT *An anonymous 12th FBS pilot pauses to have his photo taken by his crew chief before firing up his Mustang. The aircraft's load for the impending mission comprises rockets and GP bombs, which will more than likely be expended against enemy vehicles or armour on the frontline to the north of Chinhae (K-10) (Truett Smith)*

ABOVE *The 'Dogpatch' persona briefly extended all the way into North Korea, for this sign was posted at Pyongyang East Airfield (K-24) during the 18th FBG's temporary stay in October 1950 (Tom Shockley)*

RIGHT *When the 39th FIS was attached to the 18th FBW, its strength was increased to four squadrons, making it the largest UN fighter-bomber outfit in Korea – No 2 Sqn, SAAF, was also included in this powerful organisation. This 39th FIS Mustang (FF-630) has been serviced and waits for the ordnance crews to arm it up for the next mission (Karl Dittmer)*

was floundering out of his spin, but he snapped his fighter over and got his speed back up in seconds – so much so that he started a steep climb (this was due to the light weight of his fighter). This time he slacked off at the top of his loop, and followed through gently. Now the pattern was set. I was flying a tight circle on the horizontal and he elected to fly his sparring circle on the vertical, snapping at me as we passed each other. We held our turns and I looked for a break, and as he picked up speed, I saw that we were getting closer each time we closed on the south side of my circle! More and more rapidly, the two fighters got out of phase, and I was able to kick my rudder and snap a shot at him each time.

'My adversary saw his advantage slipping, and he knew that after the next pass, I would be coming in on his tail. He began to climb again, and I knew he was unnerved because when he got to the top of the loop, his aircraft wobbled somewhat. I added throttle and waited him out. He fell unevenly this time, and I cut wide for a split-second. At the bottom of the loop, he recovered and began his pull-up, but luckily my timing was good.

'I wrapped up my Mustang, and while I was still in my turn I began firing. I saw my tracers converge and pour into his wing. I eased the rudder to the right to keep him in sight. Then a puff of blue smoke spouted from his wing. He wobbled slightly and fell out of his turn. Slowly, he rolled over and went into a long glide. The plane crashed into the ground with the pilot still in the cockpit. It was an exciting kill for me, and it reminded me of the old days in World War 2. My adversary had been a Soviet-built Yak-3 flown by a very competent pilot.'

1/2 November 1950 proved to be noteworthy days, for in a little over 24 hours five Yaks fell to Mustang pilots in a flurry of engagements, the frequency of which would never be repeated for the F-51 units. Not only did Robert Thresher get credit for his Yak-3 kill, his wingman, Capt Flake, was also credited with an identical victory on the same mission. It didn't end there, however, for later that same day the 67th FBS was jumped by numerous MiG-15s. All the Mustangs emerged intact, and several of the pilots were able to claim three damaged enemy jets in return. The inexperienced MiG pilots had made the mistake of tangling with the Mustang at a very low altitude, where the F-51 could easily turn inside of them.

The following day Alma Flake added a second kill to his tally when he 'bagged' a Yak-9, whilst 1Lt James L Glessner of the 12th FBS went one better by downing a pair of Yak-9s. Despite these successes, the rules of engagement for the aerial war had effectively changed overnight with the appearance of the MiG-15, and from now on the jet fighter threat would always be out there for the fighter-bomber pilots. 'MiG Alley' would quickly prove to be no place for a slower, propeller-driven, aircraft.

PYONGYANG EVACUATION

In late November and early December, Pyongyang was not the place to be. The Mustang units, having only just arrived in the North Korean capital, and yet to unpack the boxcars full of their ground equipment, were suddenly caught in the path of the communist counter-attack. Maj Bill Myers was the maintenance chief for the

BELOW *These 67th FBS 'Red Scarf' Mustangs prepare to load up with both 500-lb GP and 1000-lb GP bombs for interdiction missions against rail and road routes that were being heavily used at night to run supplies down from Manchuria to the frontline. Note that the 1000-lb bombs all have personal messages chalked onto them (USAF)*

18th FBG at the time, and he gives some details of what those few days at Pyongyang were like;

'Right before we moved north from Pusan, we were flying long missions to hit Pyongyang West (K-23), and the cold weather was already setting in. I remember we had to preflight and post-flight our own Mustangs, and that included refuelling them from hand-pumped 50-gallon drums. We even spent a couple of nights with Col Dean Hess and his RoKAF "bunch". These strikes continued on until the latter part of the month, when we were told that we were moving up to the area that we had been bombing all this time – Pyongyang.

'We didn't get to stay long at our new base. My log book shows we were pushing hard on 30 November through to 2 December, trying to give our guys protection as they evacuated. We kept our F-51s in the air all day, as it wasn't far from our base at Pyongyang East (K-24) to where the Chinese masses were coming down the roads. It got so bad that any of our maintenance people that were not working on the aircraft were given a rifle and put out on the perimeter to defend our equipment. The only shelter available to us were some well-strafed sheds that we used as a Mess area.

Our runway was a dirt strip, with one row of lights.

'It was late in the afternoon of 5 December when I led the last four-ship flight out of K-24. My log shows I was in F-51D 44-74752. We capped the base while the last C-47 loaded the remainder of our maintenance personnel. We recovered down at Suwon AB (K-13), where the runway lighting consisted of two five-gallon oil drums at the approach-touchdown point on the south end. I remember there was a bomb crater right at the end of the runway, which didn't add to the safety factor! It was rough.

'The crew chiefs had to maintain our Mustangs, working at night with a few flashlights and a piece of canvas draped over the props to shield them from the freezing wind and snow. Fortunately, we didn't spend much time here, and soon moved into our new home at Chinhae. During those hectic days of pulling abruptly out of North Korea, our maintenance people did a magnificent job of keeping our Mustangs in the enemy's "face".'

By the end of December 1950, the 18th FBG had compiled some very impressive statistics. Since the war had begun, the group had shot down, or damaged, 16 enemy aircraft, destroyed over 1300 trucks, 190 tanks

BELOW *KARIN ANN (FF-888) gets its plexiglas windscreen wiped clean prior to the next mission. This photo was taken at Chinhae in December 1951, and unusually for this time of year, the sky is blue and there is no snow on the ground! The blue and white spinner indicates this was a 39th FIS Mustang (James Harris)*

FAR RIGHT *Lt John Lent, a 'Foxy Few' pilot from the 12th FBS, was photographed during a visit to the bomb dump at K-46 (John Lent)*

RIGHT *Lt Jake Armstrong of the 67th FBS was assigned this newly-delivered replacement Mustang that arrived from the USA with a total flying time of just 32 hours. An aircraft in such a condition was very much the exception in Korea, for most of the F-51s being flown by the Wing were very 'high timers' that required excessive maintenance to keep them serviceable for the job they were required to perform (Jake Armstrong)*

BELOW *The Mustang pilots flew the missions, but it was the maintenance people who allowed the wing to support the ground troops holding off the Chinese Army. This 67th FBS F-51D is undergoing minor maintenance at K-46 (Sam Forbert)*

and 75 locomotives – the exact quantity of rolling stock destroyed was not available. A conservative estimate of the number of enemy troops killed or wounded was 10,000+. In one day alone, the 18th caught a number of truck convoys on the narrow mountain roads leading out of Manchuria as the Chinese were trying, out of desperation, to resupply their troops and keep their initial offensive going. When the smoke cleared, 130 trucks had been destroyed, which represented ten per cent of the total for the period. This was almost certainly the first major encounter that the Chinese had had with UN fighter-bombers, and from then on supply convoys moved at night.

A NEW YEAR

The first six months of 1951 rushed past in a blur for personnel of the 18th FBG. Although the Chinese offensive had been stopped at a line close to where the war had started, and US media attention was now focused squarely on the F-86 squadrons that had been brought in to do battle with the MiG-15s, down below the high altitude duelling the war went on. At ground level there was

no glamour or mystique attached to the fighting. The F-51 had one job to do, and that was to put a stop to any supplies that were coming south. To allow the Chinese Army to launch a fresh offensive with full provisions would spell disaster for the UN 'ground pounders'.

Such was the routine adopted by the Mustang wing that the missions seemed to blend into one, as the days turned into weeks, and the weeks into months. New aircraft types were appearing on the scene, but it was still the 'old F-51' that sent the adrenaline pumping through the veins of the 'troops in the trenches' when Mustangs arrived overhead to help them out.

The 18th FBG celebrated its first anniversary in the war in July 1951. The commanding officer of the group at that time was Col Ralph H Saltsman, who had been a B-17 squadron CO during World War 2. When he assumed command of the 18th just prior to its anniversary, he completed 17 years of flying in the USAAC/ USAAF/USAF. Saltsman still vividly remembers the wild party held on 6 July 1951 to mark the one-year milestone;

'That party is etched in my memory, as the celebration didn't wind down until well after midnight. All of us

ABOVE RIGHT *Lt Max Tomich was a 67th FBS pilot, and he is seen here preflighting his fully armed F-51 on the K-46 flightline. These aircraft are parked in the ordnance area, where they have been loaded according to the requirements for the next mission – in this instance, rockets and 500-lb GP bombs (Max Tomich)*

BELOW RIGHT *Wearing his ominously decorated black helmet, with its crossed bones and beer mug, 1Lt Jack Shepard prepares to clamber aboard his 67th FBS Mustang at K-46 during the winter of 1952 (Jack Shepard)*

were doing the Zulu War Dance with the South African pilots, and before it was all over, we had pounded holes in the floor of the Officers' Club at Chinhae! It was getting to be a joke that carpenters had to show up every morning after a party to make the necessary repairs. Our fighter pilots worked hard and played hard, and overall they were a wonderful bunch of guys! We invited No 2 Sqn SAAF to stop over at Clark Air Base on their way home and visit us when the war ended, but it went on much longer than anyone would have guessed. The echoes of "Aye Ziga Zoomba" still ring in my ears!

Returning to the daily grind of flight operations, Col Saltsman recalls a mission which was flown some three weeks after the famous party;

'It was one of those days where I could sense something big was "coming down". At the time, I was down at Chinhae, so I packed my bag and tossed it in my two-place "piggy-back" Mustang and headed up to our forward base at Hoengsong (K-46). Sure enough, the operation order came through at midnight instructing us to send 64 Mustangs up to Pyongyang, which was referred to as the "hot-spot".

'We were to be part of an all-day attack by Fifth AF bombers and fighter-bombers. I was in the lead of our "gaggle", and despite very poor weather conditions, we attacked our targets with excellent results. None of the bombers made it to the target due to the weather, and only a few of the jet fighter-bombers succeeded in dropping their bombs.

'The afternoon mission had to work against even worse weather conditions. We went in with 60 F-51s, but couldn't hit the targets because everything was "socked in". We didn't lose any ships in the morning, and only one in the afternoon. By making it to the target while the others didn't, we saved the day for Fifth AF, and as a

RIGHT *LITTLE JOE was the F-51D assigned to 1Lt Joe B Dishongh of the 67th FBS. The squadron's pilots usually wore their red caps and scarf when they were relaxing at the Officers' Club, or in the Operations shack. All of their Mustangs wore the red trim (Joe Dishongh)*

BELOW *Lt Joe Dishongh (left) visits old friend Lt Jim Mitchell, who was Operations Officer for the 10th Liaison Squadron, flying L-5s out of Seoul City AP (K-16). This particular aircraft was never on any USAF inventory, for it was rebuilt from a wide variety of parts salvaged from other wrecked aircraft in the squadron. Note the Fifth AF insignia on the L-5's tail, and the No 2 Sqn, SAAF, Mustang parked behind it (Joe Dishongh)*

RIGHT No 2 Sqn, SAAF, (nicknamed the 'Flying Cheetahs') joined the war on 16 November 1950 when they flew their Mustangs into Pusan East Airfield (K-9). At this time, the 18th FBW was packing up and moving into North Korea, and the unit duly joined them in the push north. Subsequently attached to the wing for the duration of the war, the South Africans did an outstanding job with the Mustang for the entire time they flew it. This photo was taken at Suwon AB in late 1950, and aside from the two Mustangs it also reveals the tailfin of an F-84 and a departing USAF C-54 (Howard Tanner)

FAR LEFT *Sunrise at Chinhae reveals the flightline for the South African Mustangs. The aircraft in the distance have been serviced and armed for the first missions of the day. No 2 Sqn's incredible contributions to the war effort was clearly acknowledged by the USAF, who awarded its pilots no fewer than 55 Distinguished Flying Crosses (DFCs) in Korea (Roy Bell)*

LEFT *1Lt Walter H Burke poses with the '100 mission horseshoe' after he had completed his century of sorties on 12 September 1951. It took less than ten months for Burke to achieve this landmark, which was a fair indicator of just how busy the 18th FBW was at the time. The 67th FBS Mustang shown here was not Burke's assigned aircraft, for his regular mount was named 'Lady Patrick' after his wife (Walt Burke)*

result, we were told by our Wing Commander, Col T C Rogers, that he thought we were probably the best outfit he had ever been associated with in the air force.'

39TH FIS

In May 1951 the saga of the Mustang in Korea took another turn. The 39th FIS, which had flown the F-51 with its parent 35th FBG, was now left with all the group's Mustangs as its sister unit, the 40th, had pulled back to Japan to re-equip with F-80Cs. The 39th subsequently became part of the 18th FBW, shifting all of its F-51s down to Chinhae.

During the course of the war the 39th FIS enjoyed some of the most interesting experiences encountered by any unit in-theatre. They not only flew the Mustang, but in June 1952 pulled away from the 18th FBW and became part of the famous 51st FW up at Suwon, flying F-86s. This allowed the unit to produce some of the highest scoring aces of the war. Their designation of Fighter Interceptor Squadron never changed throughout the conflict, even though they were involved in the fighter-bomber role for more than half of the war. During its 37 months in the frontline, the 39th served with three different wings, and a handful of its pilots went from 'mud movers' to 'dogfighters' over 'MiG Alley'.

One of the most dangerous, and costly, missions flown by the 18th FBW took place on 14 August 1951 against targets in Pyongyang. Again weather conditions on the run in to the North Korean capital were terrible, and the Mustang pilots also encountered heavy anti-aircraft fire at tree-top level. A widely published black and white photograph taken during this mission shows Mustangs dropping napalm tanks right over the smoke stacks in the

LEFT 1Lt Mario Prevosti (left) was a pilot with the 12th FBS, and he is seen here taking 'time out' to have his picture taken in front of his loaded F-51 with one of the many South Korean 'houseboys' that were employed by some of the pilots in the squadron. This photo was taken at Chinhae in 1951 (Mario Prevosti)

BELOW When this photo was taken in December 1952, the Mustang was just entering its thirtieth month of combat in Korea, thus making it the 'top timer' of any fighter-bomber type in its class. Photographed at K-46 about six weeks before the 67th FBS flew its Mustangs over to the new base at Osan (K-55), where they traded them in for the new F-86F, Old Hosenose was one of the last F-51s in 18th FBW's inventory (Bill Fillmann)

RIGHT *In early July 1952 the 18th FBW reached another milestone when its completed its 45,000th sortie. On the left is the pilot that flew the mission, Capt Elliott D Ayer, of the 67th FBS. Two weeks later, he was killed on his 84th mission. On the far right is the 18th FBW's Commander, Col William H Clark (Sam Forbert)*

BELOW *One of the most unique Mustangs to emerge from the war, this particular aircraft was built from parts of other wrecked F-51s salvaged from the Chinhae 'boneyard'. Not recorded on the USAF's inventory list, it was flown by the 18th's Maintenance Chief, Maj Bill Myers. The fighter's trademark was its 'Bumble Bee' spinner (Milt Tarr)*

LEFT *Final preparations are made to the wing CO's F-51 prior to the pilot arriving on the flightline following his brief on the targets for the up and coming mission. Judging by the colour of the helmet being placed on the windscreen framing, the CO's Mustang was to be flown by a member of the 12th FBS. The aircraft was armed with both rockets and bombs (David Bickel)*

BELOW
In almost every USAF combat squadron that served in Korea, the wing commander had his own assigned aircraft, even though it was mostly flown by other pilots. This F-51D was the 18th FBW's example, and it carries the wing emblem and command stripes which represented the colours of all three USAF squadrons then flying under its control. This photo was taken when Lt Col Albert J Freund was the incumbent CO (David Bickel)

LEFT *If the NKPAF or Chinese air force had had air superiority, they would have had no trouble pinpointing the Operations buildings for the 12th and 67th FBSs and No 2 Sqn, SAAF! This colourful view was taken at the 18th FBW's forward staging base at Hoengsong (K-46) (Bruce Clark)*

ABOVE *CONNIE, a 67th FBS F-51D, is seen slowly taxying out as part of a three-ship flight. Its mission on this occasion required only 500-lb GP bombs and the standard load of 0.50-cal ammo. When flying out of K-46, the Mustang was in easy range of 'MiG Alley', and its lucrative targets, but due to the heavy 'Triple-A' and the constant MiG-15 threat, most of missions into the area were left to the F-84s with F-86 escorts (Don Hallowell)*

RIGHT *These newly-arrived replacement Mustangs were photographed at Chinhae just hours after they had flown in from Japan. In a matter of days, they would carry the colours of the squadrons they had been assigned to. Indeed, the F-51 second from the end has already received its sharksmouth, but does not yet carry any trim colours (Steven Levandoski)*

industrial section of the city. Despite the squadrons involved having to deal both with poor weather and intense flak, the mission proved to be one of the most precisely executed of the whole war.

Some 60 Mustangs (all four squadrons from the 18th Wing) were involved, with the lead aircraft of the 67th FBS being flown by 1Lt Walter H Burke;

'Before we could get in to the targets with our ordnance, we had to negotiate some of the worst weather I had seen. We were on a strict time table, so the navigation had to be perfect.

'We arrived over the initial point (IP) exactly on schedule, and in a matter of seconds we were heavily engaged by some of the most accurate and intense anti-aircraft fire I had ever seen! This persisted all the way to, and through, the attack route. On top of this we had other problems. The close proximity of hospital sites and a Prisoner of War compound to our assigned targets made pinpoint navigation an absolute necessity. We came in on our targets at treetop level with our weapon of choice – napalm.

'The explosions and fire created by the initial hits made it easier for the flights of F-51s that were coming in behind us. Post-strike recce pictures confirmed that we

had destroyed ten warehouse type buildings, taken out one automatic weapons position and damaged several other buildings. We lost one pilot – Maj Bill Green, who was the 67th's Operations Officer. He had been flying at the tail end of the formation.'

1Lt Burke was awarded the First Oak Leaf Cluster in lieu of an additional Distinguished Flying Cross for this mission.

Pyongyang was struck again that same afternoon, but this time three pilots were lost – all from the 39th. The unit came in right over the smoke stacks, and amongst those killed was squadron commander, Maj Murrit Davis. The results of the afternoon strike were excellent, however. Nine months previous to this infamous mission over Pyongyang, these same aircraft had been operating from bases that were now their targets.

By the summer of 1951 it seemed that the 18th FBW was reaching some type of milestone every week, proving that the days of the propeller-driven fighter-bomber were far from over when it came to executing the close air support mission. Reinforcing this were the Corsairs and Skyraiders of the US Navy and Marine Corps, and the Sea Furies and Fireflies of the Royal Navy's Fleet Air Arm.

The first major milestone reached by the 18th

BELOW *This 12th FBS Mustang was flown against the rampant NKPA during the early days of the war. It is parked at Pusan AB (K-9), and its ordnance load comprises napalm and rockets. Many lucrative targets were available to Mustang pilots during this time as the frontline moved ever closer to the F-51 base (Harry Moreland)*

RIGHT *The heavy snows that covered Hoengsong in December 1952 were to be the last that the F-51 would have to endure. Less than a month after this photo was taken, the aircraft flew their last missions of the war. This unusual photo of a personalised HE bomb was taken by the crew chief of this F-51D (George Banasky)*

FAR RIGHT ABOVE *Many of the F-51s that sustained heavy battle damage over their targets were able to fly (or glide) the short distance back to base, but not all made it down safely. Flak damage often forced pilots to crash-land their stricken fighters, or resulted in the undercarriage failing on touchdown. This South African Mustang lost much of its starboard wing and various engine panels whilst grinding to a halt, but its pilot walked away from the wreck (Vern Burke)*

FAR RIGHT BELOW *Most of the F-51s that were parked down at Chinhae were either in various stages of repair, or replacement aircraft waiting to be sent up to Hoengsong (K-46) to fly combat missions. This Mustang has just received its new sharksmouth, and is ready for action – Lt Dale Backman would fly its first few missions (Dale Backman)*

occurred on 30 August 1951, when the wing logged its 25,000th combat sortie – just one year and one day after the 18th FBG had flown its first mission over Korea. The pilot that was credited with flying the milestone sortie was Capt Winn A Coomer of the 67th FBS. This 'pegged' the wing as the first FEAF unit to 'hit' the 25,000 mark.

Contrary to popular belief, not all of these sorties were flown with ordnance destined to be expended against enemy tanks, trucks and bunkers. When a Mustang pilot went down, every effort was made to assist the SAR flight sent in to recover him. There were some sad tales to be told of failed attempts, but a fair proportion of the rescue missions launched were successful. One of these is related here by Capt Robert A Nolan, who flew with the 67th FBS;

'One cold day during the winter of 1951-52, my flight was assigned duty as ResCap alert in support of a large gaggle attacking a target in the vicinity of Hamhung, on the east coast of North Korea.

ABOVE South Korean labour filled many voids in the day-to-day operation of the 18th FBW, and although most individuals had jobs within the buildings on the base, a select group were allowed to shuttle parts back and forth to the flightline, as well as perform assembly work on the rockets and napalm tanks. This view shows Korean workers delivering belted 0.50-cal ammunition for a 67th FBS F-51 parked on the flightline at K-46 (Ted Hanna)

RIGHT The main maintenance hangar at Chinhae was always a hive of activity, being filled with Mustangs in various stages of repair. In this case, a few of the Mustangs have had to be pushed outside to be worked on because of a lack of floor space in the hangar. The two Mustangs further from the camera were assigned to the 12th FBS and 39th FIS respectively (Milt Tarr)

LEFT *Two flights of F-51s from the 39th FIS 'Blinker Nose' squadron line up for rearming in an effort to keep the turn around time to a minimum. This photo was taken in late 1951, by which time the frontline had stabilised somewhat. The Chinese were in the process of attempting a major offensive in the wake of the first snow in an effort to win ground before the hard winter set in. In response to this push, these Mustangs were over the frontline several times a day (Glen Wold)*

BELOW *Graduation day for the RoK Military Academy at Chinhae (K-10), with Mustangs from the 12th FBS providing a suitable backdrop across the runway. The mountainous scenery in the area during the spring and summer months was a photographer's dream. These ceremonies were presided over by 18th Wing Commander, Col T C Rogers (Steven Levandoski)*

RIGHT *With their responsibilities in the Korean War coming to an end, these tired Mustangs wait for their final flight back to Japan in January 1953. This photo was taken at the new 'super base' at Osan (K-55) right before the 67th gave up their F-51s for F-86Fs (Ralph Costenbader)*

BELOW *A large group of 67th FBS pilots line up to have their picture taken while decked out in full winter flying gear in late 1952. The unit had just started to wind down their Mustang operations, although their mission load remained heavy right to the end (Damon Reeder)*

'That afternoon we received word that one of the attacking aircraft was down, so we launched. It was one from the 39th FIS, a sister-squadron to the 67th. We carried external fuel tanks which would allow us to remain in the area while rescue efforts were under way.

'When we arrived on the scene, the covering aircraft – which were now low on fuel – stated that they had seen the pilot moving around, and that enemy troops were at the base of the mountain. As we got word that a helicopter had just been launched from a carrier off shore, the attack aircraft headed for our base at K-46. Moments later, we also got word that MiGs were launching from Antung, so evidently they were going to try and hamper our efforts. On top of that, the weather was turning lousy and it was getting darker by the minute.

'I decided it would be best if I headed for the 'copter and guided him back here as fast as possible. As I was en route, we were notified that due to the weather, it had aborted the mission. We resumed station over our downed comrade as darkness covered the terrain below. We would have to go back to base and hope that he could evade until first light.

'Usually on combat missions during winter months, I carried an air force issue parka under the seat. I thought that by having it, if I went down I'd have extra protection from the weather. An idea struck me that I could fly low over the downed pilot's position and drop it to him. I notified the rest of my flight to maintain altitude while I dropped down to treetop level. I set the Mustang up for a slow pass and rolled the canopy back. When I was over

LEFT *A view of Chinhae (K-10) from the summit of an overlooking mountain top. This base, which had been a major Japanese seaplane facility during World War 2, served as the main HQ of the 18th FBW until it moved north to Osan (Russ Bunn)*

RIGHT *The 12th FBS got their 'teeth sunk into' many targets during the unit's 30 months of combat with the Mustang. These fully-loaded Mustangs are sat ready for action at of Seoul City Airport (K-16) on 6 September 1951 (Boardman Reed)*

BELOW
A combination of South African and American groundcrewmen swarm all over this SAAF Mustang as it is made ready for another sortie. When the Chinese entered the war, and the 18th FBG had to pull its squadrons out of Pyongyang in a hurry, the busy staging area at Seoul City became the key facility for fast reloads of ordnance and quick turnaround times. Note the bomb-damaged hangar in the background (Ed Nebinger)

BELOW This scene resembles a landscape painting, with lush green hillsides, blue sky and a dozen Mustangs lined up on the ramp. Actually, this was No 2 Sqn's dispersal area at Chinhae AB. The F-51s are being loaded with ordnance for the numerous missions that the squadron had been scheduled to complete that day. This photo was taken in the late summer of 1951, by which time the 18th FBW had set up their permanent HQ at K-10 (Milt Tarr)

the spot I thought he was hiding, I threw the parka overboard. We reformed the flight and proceeded back to K-46.

'The next day, we received word that the pilot, Capt Fred Wade, had been rescued at first light. A few days later, I went over to 39th FIS Operations to congratulate the pilot. I asked him if he had gotten the parka I dropped. He said he saw it leave the aircraft, and for a split-second he thought I had bailed out! But, when first light came, he saw it on the ground and retrieved it. He gave it back to me as a gift, and to this day, it still hangs in my closet as a reminder of a mission I will never forget!'

The war continued into 1952, and for the 18th FBW, things remained as active as ever – despite the dearth of reporting in the US press about their exploits. Combat losses amongst pilots in the wing remained high, the list of pilots breaking the 100-mission mark steadily grew, and the attrition rate for the now war-weary Mustangs continued to rise. By the end of June, the 18th had flown its 45,000th sortie – this figure alone illustrates exactly how active the wing had been. Despite this stunning statistic, F-86 units tangling with MiGs 'over the Yalu' continued to grab the headlines back in America.

The 'top brass' within Fifth AF had, by no means, chosen to ignore the 18th FBW, however, as the pressure was still on them to 'keep the heat' on the communists. With the F-84 and F-80 being used to perform the lion's share of the ground attack missions into 'MiG Alley', the senior men at Fifth AF HQ focused their attention on what was happening over, and immediately beyond, the frontline. Lt Ted Hanna remembers some 'heat' that filtered down to unit level during his tour;

'It was during the summer of 1952, and we were briefed to fly a group "gaggle" up to a mining area north-east of Sinanju. The strike force consisted of about 20 Mustangs loaded with 500-lb GP bombs and 0.50-cal ammo. This mission was potentially more dangerous than operating over the frontline, for we were heading into the MiG-15's "hunting ground", and so required an escort of F-86s.

'Our Mustangs were flying at 10,000 ft and our MiGCap was above us at 20,000 ft. The leader of the Sabres was none other than Maj "Bones" Marshall (the sixth highest-scoring ace in Korea). Shortly after passing Sinanju, Fifth AF broadcast "the trains are leaving the station", which meant the MiGs had taken off from

BELOW *The 18th FBW's forward staging base at K-46 was well protected by AA emplacements, which had a clear view of any enemy aircraft that might have tried to attack the scores of Mustangs typically parked on the ramp – the base also contained one of the biggest bomb dumps in South Korea. Fortunately, most of the nocturnal harassment raids pulled off by the bi-plane Po-2s were centred around Suwon AB, where the F-86s were located (Sam Forbert)*

Capt Daniel 'Chappie' James rests for a minute by his Mustang, which has already been reloaded for its next sortie. This photo was taken at Taegu during the fight to save the 'Pusan Perimeter'. There is no mistaking which squadron 'Chappie' flew for, as the 12th's sharksmouth is clearly visible. A member of the original 'Dallas' Squadron that came over from the Philippines, 'Chappie' remained in the USAF postwar and later became the first black officer to achieve the rank of four-star general (Ed Nebinger)

BELOW *Loaded with napalm, these 67th FBS Mustangs were photographed whilst en route to attack enemy troops located by a FAC. The enemy could not defend itself against a napalm attack except by sheltering inside deeply buried underground bunkers (Frank Harvan)*

RIGHT *Capt Robert A Nolan was one of the many 67th FBS pilots that came to the unit with prior combat experience gained during World War 2. He is seen posing alongside his 'seasonal gifts' for the enemy. This photo was taken immediately prior to launching on a Christmas Day 1951 sortie over North Korea. Nolan flew 100 missions with the squadron before moving to the 40th FIS at Johnson AB, Japan, where he continued to fly the Mustang (Robert Nolan)*

Antung and were headed our way. Immediately following this transmission, the F-86s dropped their external fuel tanks, which fell right through our formation! Luckily no one got hit by them. Moments later the fight started! The MiGs came at us from below and flew straight up through our formation, firing as they went. At this point, we got in trail formation and made our bomb runs. After we had dropped our ordnance, we formed up for the flight home. Paul Kniss's Mustang was hit by cannon from one of the MiGs, and he bailed out and was taken prisoner.

'Well, Fifth AF HQ got "bent out of shape" because we had lost a pilot even with plenty of F-86 cover. The Sabre people in turn claimed we were "off course". When we told them that their drop tanks had fallen through our formation, their faces turned red! There were fingers being pointed at everybody. Finally, Fifth AF sent an "expert" down to show us how to fly the mission. That went over like a lead balloon. The colonel that was sent down to straighten us out was from an F-84 wing. From what I understand, he had flown the Mustang in World War 2. On his first interdiction mission with us, he forgot to burn down his fuselage tank before making the bomb

run. You know what happened – his aircraft snapped twice and he augured straight into the ground. That was the last interference we ever had concerning our mission, and how to fly it.'

By the autumn of 1952, the North American Aviation production lines were rolling at full tilt on the new F-86F. First in the queue to receive these aircraft were the fighter interceptor squadrons, and once their requirements had been satisfied, plans were being made to use the new Sabre in the close support role. This at last set the stage for the Mustang's retirement from combat, with the decision being made to replace all of the F-80s and F-51s in Korea with F-86Fs. This change would move close air support into a new high-mach era, and with the completion of the new 'super base' at Osan-ni (K-55), the 18th FBW would have the perfect home for their new aircraft. As the only unit in-theatre still flying the F-80C, the 8th FBW would remain at Suwon (K-13).

The 18th FBW set many records in the first 30 months of the war, and they had done it in an 'all-jet' environment with a piston-engined aircraft that had not been designed to do what it was being asked to do! By

LEFT *Four Mustang pilots from the same 67th FBS flight pose impatiently for the camera, prior to their taking off on another mission over Korea. This shot was taken at the 18th FBW's forward staging base at K-46. At this time, the wing was flying the majority of its missions over the frontline, and immediately beyond. Mustangs of the 67th were always trimmed in red (Warren Mills)*

the time they were ready to fly the remaining F-51s back to Japan, the wing had easily topped the 50,000 mission mark. A large number of Mustang pilots from the 18th transitioned onto jets, and went on to enjoy long careers with the USAF in both war and peace. However, despite their longevity of service or seniority in rank, the 'Mustang Men' of the 18th formed a close-knit fraternity of 'brothers in arms' that has only be separated over the ensuing years by death.

18TH FBW 'FIRSTS' IN THE KOREAN WAR

1. The first American air unit to have a member receive the Medal of Honor. Maj Lou Sebille, mortally wounded, deliberately crashed his F-51 into an enemy armoured vehicle on 5 August 1950

2. The first to fly combat missions from airstrips north of the 38th Parallel

3. The first to encounter the MiG-15 in combat over North Korea

4. The first to form a true United Nations Air Wing, when the South African Air Force's No 2 Sqn joined them in November 1950

5. The first wing to reach 45,000 combat sorties during the Korean War. The 18th FBW had logged this total by mid-July 1952

RIGHT *An F-51 returns from a mission over North Korea in the early autumn of 1952. In the background is the familiar landmark, 'Old Papasan Mountain'. At this time, the 12th FBS was still operating from two bases in South Korea, with the most used of the pair being K-46 (Harlon Hain)*

BELOW *Capt J D DeBruler enjoys some 'down time' on the flightline at Chinhae AB, having just returned from yet another sortie. DeBruler was the 18th FBG's Adjutant at the time this photo was taken (Ralph Saltsman)*

LEFT *F-51D 44-73912 is shown in 18th FBG colours, with squadron stripes and a wing emblem painted forward of the cockpit. Its red trim indicates that Old Hosenose was assigned to the 67th FBS. This shot was taken in late 1952, just as the Mustang's career started to wind down (Doug Carter)*

BELOW *18th FBW CO, Brig Gen T C Rogers (left), and 18th FBG commander Col Ralph Saltsman (centre) present an award to Maj Colson in October 1951. Note the 'Fighting Cock' squadron emblem which was painted on most of the 67th FBS's Mustangs. Rogers' career in the USAAC began in the late 1930s, while Saltsman commanded a B-17 squadron during World War 2 (Dale Backman)*

FAR LEFT *Maintenance chief, Maj Bill Myers (left), is joined by Maj Milt Tarr (centre) and an anonymous officer in a group shot taken in front of their prized possession – F-51D FF-800 – behind the maintenance hanger at Chinhae. The 18th FMS, under the supervision of Maj Tarr, assembled this Mustang from several battle damaged aircraft at K-10. The enlisted members of the squadron presented it to Myers as a birthday gift, since he didn't have a wing aircraft assigned to him. The Mustang also carried the major's name on its canopy rail (Milt Tarr)*

LEFT *The tower at 'Dogpatch' (K-10) was kept constantly busy with traffic shuttling between Chinhae and Hoengsong. There were also several cargo flights per day bringing in supplies and spare parts from Japan (Milt Tarr)*

BELOW *A group of 12th FBS pilots enjoy a break from the flying at the 18th FBW's forward staging base at K-46. With no R&R facilities in-theatre, everyone was pretty well restricted to the base. 'Foxy Few' pilots were easy to spot, with their yellow caps (John Lent)*

ABOVE *The end of a magnificent era! This group of 67th FBS pilots flew the very last USAF F-51 combat mission in Korea – note how the flight gear had changed from the early days. All three of the Mustang squadrons that were flying under 18th FBW control would stand down and convert over to the F-86F Sabre at Osan Air Base (K-55) (Joe Ortega)*

RIGHT *ROTATION BLUES was a 67th FBS Mustang, and it is seen here loaded with five-in rockets and two 500-lb GP bombs ready for its next assignment over enemy territory. Most of squadron aircraft carried names painted on both sides of the nose, the left side usually being named by the pilot, and the right side by the crew chief or armourer (Sam Forbert)*

Chapter Five

TACTICAL RECONNAISSANCE OVER KOREA

When the Korean War broke out, the UN crucially needed both tactical and strategic reconnaissance to monitor the progress of the NKPA. However, due to the veritable 'blackout' of North Korea since the end of World War 2, little information was available. The solution to this problem was to send a number of photo-recce aircraft over the 38th Parallel and obtain photographs of the communist country. However, there was a near void of suitable aircraft types in the Far East – on 25 June 1950, FEAF possessed a grand total of one photo-jet squadron (flying RF-80As) and one gun camera lab. To say that this area had been allowed to lapse into almost total obscurity since the end of the Pacific War would be an understatement.

A call immediately went out to HQ USAF, who responded by urgently flying in two squadrons – the 162nd Tactical Reconnaissance Squadron (night photo) and the 363rd Reconnaissance Technical Squadron. They did not arrive in Japan until August, however.

The parent organisation for the tactical reconnais-sance mission during the Korean War would be the 67th TRW, which would utilise the facilities at Kimpo (K-14) as their main headquarters. As a wing, they would use four different aircraft types to carry out the mission, namely the RB-26, RF-80, RF-86 and the RF-51. Of the three squadrons that executed their orders, only one would be involved with the Mustang.

On 3 September 1950, the 45th TRS was activated at Itazuke AB, Japan. This order initially provoked little action, and it took some months for the squadron to be brought up to full strength. The sole recce unit that had been based in Japan was the 8th TRS, and when the 67th TRW took over the tactical recce role, this unit changed its designation to the 15th TRS. They did, however, retain their RF-80As.

Fifth AF had tasked the 67th TRW with an enormous responsibility, and they picked one of the most capable individuals in the USAF to whip the unit into fighting shape – Col Karl L 'Pop' Polifka. His first order of business was to assign each of the squadrons a specific job, and to

RIGHT *A mix of straight F-51Ds and RF-51Ds was the standard complement for the 45th TRS. During their early combat operations they were based at Taegu (K-2). Their speciality was visual reconnaissance over the frontline and enemy supply routes (Boardman C Reed)*

make sure everything was well co-ordinated with the Eighth Army command. The 15th TRS (RF-80) was assigned coverage of enemy airfields and supply routes by day, these targets usually calling for missions to be flown deep into North Korea – the 12th TRS (RB-26) would handle the same mission as the 15th, only at night. Finally, the 45th TRS covered the frontline with visual and photographic reconnaissance.

During the early days of the 45th's tenure in Korea, the unit operated out of Taegu because the frontline were so fluid – they could easily cover the front from coast to coast from this site. The squadron flew a mixture of straight F-51Ds and RF-51Ds, the conversion for the latter aircraft being carried out in Japan. Due to the limited number of Mustangs available, regular D-models always outnumbered the specialist 'RFs'. Although the 45th was activated in early September, they did not get their first RF-51s until sometime in November due to the complex nature of the conversions.

The squadron rewrote the textbook on tactics to be used by tactical recce squadrons – especially for those still using slower World War 2 vintage aircraft types. Early in March 1951 a new tactic was initiated by the 45th TRS that was geared to help jet fighter-bombers that possessed only limited loiter time for overflying suspected enemy targets. On the basis of night sightings (by RB-26s and Marine nightfighters) that were reported to the Joint Operations Centre, the 45th could project the probable locations that this traffic would have moved to up to first light – they based their calculations on an average speed of ten miles per hour.

At dawn, the squadron's Mustangs would take off for these areas on what became known as a 'Circle-10' mission. The recce pilots would cover a ten-mile radius of the estimated position of the targets, and even though these vehicles had been hastily camouflaged, a large number were spotted by the well-trained eyes of the Mustang pilots. At that time, they would call in the F-80s and F-84s to destroy the 'hidden' trucks. This tactic soon proved to be very successful.

The combination of low altitude work and the Mustang's vulnerability to ground fire brought about some changes in the single ship missions. Beginning 15 April 1951, all of the 45th's sorties were carried out in a two-ship configuration. This permitted one pilot to survey the ground, while the second flew higher and kept a sharp eye out for ground fire. With heavy losses being inflicted by Fifth AF fighter-bombers around the clock, the Chinese started bringing in mobile flak batteries to accompany the truck columns.

Things got so dangerous for the low-flying Mustangs, that on numerous missions they worked in flights of four, stacked up at different altitudes. This meant that four sets of eyes were now watching for any signs of heavy fire from the ground. 'Triple-A' accompanying high value assets moving south proved to be so effective that from

LEFT *Retired South Korean farmers satisfy their curiosity by taking a look at a heavily damaged Mustang from the 45th TRS near the village of Chungu. The unit's P-51Ds often absorbed heavy groundfire on their low-level recce sorties, and it got so bad that in the spring of 1951 the squadron was forced to change its tactics and raise the altitude of these missions (Bill Disbrow)*

mid-1951 onwards even day jet fighter-bombers had to alter their tactics.

As a result of outstanding accomplishments that all three squadrons achieved between 25 January and 21 April 1951, the 67th TRG was awarded a Battle Honors Unit Citation, signed by the Secretary of the Air Force and endorsed by the President. This was awarded essentially for critical photography of vital enemy targets, this imagery in turn being rapidly passed on to the fighter-bomber squadrons.

The missions flown to gain these photos ranged from frontline overflights to deep penetration sorties all the way up to the Manchurian border. The 45th TRS produced most of the coverage of enemy positions in the frontline, as well as all supply routes running north from this point up to a distance of 50 miles. The 15th TRS took the daylight recce from that point on, flying all the way up to the Yalu River, where they often met with aggressive resistance from the MiG-15s out of Antung. The remaining 12th TRS did all of the night work for the entire route. Total sorties flown during this period amounted to about 2000 flights, and resulted in a high destroyed vehicle count, along with an estimated 500 enemy troops killed. Lt Joe R Hurst recalls the 'mechanics' of a successful recce mission, followed up by leading the fighter-bombers to the target;

'We would work intermediate distances north of the frontline in the hope of spotting some lucrative enemy positions and equipment. The low man of the element would work down right over the treetops. In that position, we were very vulnerable to ground fire, but you had to get low to spot anything that the enemy had camouflaged. In one case we spotted a large group of T-34 tanks – probably a dozen.

'We marked the location on our map and returned to the closest base to refuel – Seoul City AP (K-16). While waiting for my aircraft to be readied, I briefed two flights (eight aircraft) of South Africans and two flights of 67th FBS pilots. All of these guys were flying F-51s with the 18th FBW.

'The Mustangs were loaded with 500-lb GP bombs. We led these guys up to the hidden tanks three times. The first wave of aircraft in hit all of the "Triple-A" emplacements that were protecting this group of tanks. The rest of them swarmed in and destroyed a large number of the tanks and took out all the ground fire. When the dust had settled it was dark, and a total of 32 Mustangs had put their ordnance into the area. It had been one of the longest days that I can remember.'

This had been a great example of how the Mustangs operated – similar to the FAC 'Mosquitos', but with much more speed and deadly force!

BELOW Lt Walt Elflein taxies up to the 45th's Operations building for the impending celebration of his 100th, and final, mission. This photo was taken at Kimpo AB in April 1952 (Walt Elflein)

LEFT *The 45th TRS was officially known as the 'Polka Dot' squadron, and it was one of the most colourful Mustang units in Korea. Seen here at Kimpo in 1952 is squadron pilot 1 Lt G J Isbell, with his matching flight helmet (Stanley Newman)*

On 25 May 1951, Capt Maurice Nordlund was leading a two-ship RF-51 mission in search of any hidden enemy equipment and supplies. They were operating at low altitude and working within a ten-mile radius of where the convoy should have parked for the day. After a few sweeps in the area, the target was spotted by Nordlund. He counted six trucks, a fuel supply dump and about 40 troops.

Once the enemy realised that they had been discovered, they threw up a hail of automatic weapons fire, and Nordlund's Mustang absorbed numerous hits. He elected to remain in the area until the fighter-bombers arrived, directing them to score several hits on the enemy position. The end result was the total destruction of the truck and fuel dump. This had been Nordlund's 78th combat mission with the 45th, and for his efforts he was awarded an Oak Leaf Cluster to his Distinguished Flying Cross.

On 1 July 1951, tragedy struck the 67th TRW when Col Polifka was killed in an F-51 on a dangerous combat mission up in the Kaesong area that he had insisted on

flying himself. Maj Boardman C Reed was probably the last officer to talk with Polifka. The major had been the commanding officer at Kangnung (K-18), and had come over to the 67th on their Wing Maintenance Staff. He was attached to the 45th TRS, and flew the test hops on the aircraft after they had been worked on. He vividly remembers that day in July;

'On 1 July, I was scheduled for a brief test hop in one of our F-51Ds that had just undergone a rudder change. According to my flight log, it was AF 44-74638 (FF-638). Col Polifka had scheduled himself for a particularly dangerous mission in an area that was heavily defended with "Triple-A", and this Mustang was the one he was to fly.

'At 1545 hours, I made a short flight up to 5500 ft, did several sharp turns and manoeuvres at 250 mph. I was back on the ramp in about 15 minutes. "Pop" was waiting for me, parachute slung over his shoulder. I quickly signed the Form 1-A, while the crew chief topped off the tanks. At the time I didn't realise it, but I had just performed the last landing that FF-638 would ever make!

BELOW *When the first 45th TRS pilot to reach the 100 mission mark landed safely, the entire squadron took 'time out' to celebrate. This photo was taken at a beer party for the enlisted ranks on this occasion, and everyone enjoyed the 'down' time (James Cultrona)*

LEFT The demand placed on the 45th TRS was unusually heavy due to the Chinese constantly attempting to move supplies down from the north. As a result, the night intruding USAF B-26s and Marine F4U-5Ns and F7F-3Ns took a heavy toll on all traffic after dark, and the enemy would hastily camouflage these damaged vehicles before daylight. The 45th, in turn, would be up at dawn trying to spot them, and when they did locate targets, the fighter-bombers would be called in. All of these 'Polka Dot' pilots finished their quota of 100 missions in the same week (Walt Elflein)

LEFT *LINDA and BOBBY Jr was easy to spot due to its distinctive Confederate Flag painted on its nose. This shot was taken at Kimpo on 3 September 1951 – note the lack of a hardened surface or PSP in the parking area (Boardman C Reed)*

RIGHT *1Lt Frank Trimmier has finished his mission briefing and gathered up all of his flight gear. This was taken just minutes before he took off for another low level recce hop over the frontline and supply routes. FF-735, alias MARI LOU, was assigned to the 45th TRS as a straight F-51D, armed with 0.50-cal machine guns rather than cameras (James Cultrona)*

Col Polifka flew north to his target area. His F-51 was critically hit by intense ground fire in the radiator coolant area, which was its most vulnerable spot. When 'Pop' bailed out, somehow his parachute fouled in the tail assembly and he was tragically dragged to his death. No further details are known, but it was a tremendous loss to all of us!'

Col Polifka was immediately replaced by Col Vincent Howard as Wing Commander. This was an interim move to plug the hole left by Polifka' death, for on 31 October 1951 seasoned World War 2 combat veteran, Col Edwin

S Chickering, was brought in to run the 67th TRW. One of the first observations noted by Chickering was the fact that the 45th TRS was heavily tasked, yet had only a limited number of war-weary aircraft. They had been using the F/RF-51Ds for so long that the maintenance personnel were having difficulty in keeping the majority of them in the air. Col Chickering was instrumental in gradually transitioning the 'Polka Dot' squadron over to the RF-80, allowing the unit to retire its last RF-51 well before the war had ended.

RIGHT *Pilots from the 45th TRS line up for the presentation of awards and medals. At the time, the squadron was still operating from Taegu (K-2), and the number of sorties being put up by the unit was extremely high. By the third week of April 1952, the 45th had flown its 9000th sortie (Ed Haws)*

LEFT *OU-KAY II (44-84835) was one of the 'straight' F-51Ds that was converted into an 'RF' model in Japan after the war had started. Most of the Mustangs flown by the 45th TRS were standard D-models, as the 'RFs' were only available in very limited numbers. This shot was taken at Taegu on 3 July 1951 (Boardman C Reed)*

Chapter Six

THE RoKAF

When World War 2 ended, total confusion reigned within the new democracy that had been initiated in South Korea. Without heavy financial aid from the United States, the new government in the south would never have survived, and their military force was almost non-existent. While Gen MacArthur was still overseeing the occupation of Japan, President Syngman Rhee asked the newly-retired General Claire Chennault to work up a proposal for a fledgling air force. These plans were drawn up for a 99-aircraft force, which included 25 F-51 Mustangs.

This plan was presented to Gen MacArthur and he rejected it. His reasons were twofold – firstly, a strong army was to receive priority, for it was needed by the government of the Republic of Korea in order to maintain internal order, and secondly, the communist leadership in North Korea might mistake the creation of an air force as an aggressive arms build-up in the democratic south.

In April 1950, the entire RoKAF numbered just 187 officers and 1672 enlisted men. Of the 57 pilots that were listed, only 39 were considered to be properly trained. This force was not capable of defending itself even against

RIGHT As the war entered 1953, the RoKAF would end up being the only military unit still flying Mustangs in combat. The primary base used by the Korean Mustangs was Kangnung (K-18) (Kenneth Koon)

RIGHT *In late 1951 the RoKAF begun operating out of Kangnung airfield with their F-51D Mustangs. Although the aircraft they inherited had been all but worn out by the USAF, they did a credible job in keeping them in the air. Since this base was on the east coast of South Korea, they worked a large number of targets directly north along the coast of North Korea. This RoKAF Mustang, parked at K-18, is loaded with GP bombs and rockets (John Corrigan)*

the weakest of threats, for their inventory showed just eight L-4s, five L-5s and three T-6s – a grand total of 16 aircraft, none of which could be used effectively in a combat situation. Of the ten or so airfields constructed by the Japanese in South Korea during World War 2, only two were considered to be in a 'kept up' condition – Kimpo and Seoul.

If the UN forces had not stepped in, South Korea would have fallen in just a matter of days. Intelligence reports from the June 1950 period indicate that the NKPA had close to 100,000 troops that were considered to be well trained. This equated to eight infantry divisions. On the other hand, the RoK Army had 65,000 troops, and while they were trained, they had no armour or artillery to support them.

This same Intel report stated that the NKAF had 170 aircraft, most of which were Soviet-built World War 2 types. The breakdown was as follows – 62 Il-10s, 70 Yak-3s, 22 Yak-18 transports and eight Po-2 trainers.

Most of the North Korean aircraft were based either at Pyongyang or Yonpo when the war commenced. The advisor to the North Korean military could have never dreamt that in a matter of two weeks, most of these aircraft would have been destroyed on the ground and the airfields would be cratered from one end to the other. The primary 'culprits' were the F-51s and F-80s.

During the early weeks of the war, the RoKAF was given ten Mustangs to begin building up their air force to fighting strength. The first RoK pilots to receive training did so at the hands of instructor pilots from the 36th FBS at Itazuke AB, in Japan. With F-51s in very short supply, the South Koreans took only a few down to Chinhae to begin training for eventual combat. Sadly, few details were recorded on the extensive use of the Mustang by the RoKAF during the war.

Once they received enough F-51s to form a squadron, the Koreans flew many missions out of numerous bases in South Korea, including Pyongyang during the big push toward the Yalu – the two bases that they operated out of the most were Sachon (K-4) and Kangnung (K-18). When the war ended in July 1953, most of the F-51s that had been turned in by the 18th FBW in January 1953 made their way to K-18 from Japan. Indeed, the numbers of surplus Mustangs that became available during this period were so great that some aircraft were brought back to Japan and sent instead to the Philippines.

North American F-51 (P-51D) Mustang

1. Hamilton Standard constant speed propeller 11 ft 2 in diameter (3.4038 metres)
2. Spinner
3. Propeller hub pitch change mechanism
4. Armoured ring behind spinner backplate
5. Propeller governor
6. Coolant header tank
7. Carburettor air intake
8. Starboard mainwheel
9. Filtered air intake
10. Generator
11. Rolls-Royce/Packard Merlin V-1650-7 V-twelve engine
12. Exhaust stubs
13. Fabricated engine bearer
14. Intake ducting
15. Fuel filter
16. Carburettor
17. Supercharger
18. Engine boost controller
19. Aftercooler
20. Engine oil tank, capacity 10.25 Imp gal (12.3 US gal, 46.6 lit)
21. Oil filler cap
22. Detachable engine cowling panels
23. Starboard Browning MG 53-2 0.5-in (12.7 mm) machine gun installation
24. 5-in (12.7 cm) HVAR rockets, maximum load 10
25. Wing stringers
26. Wing skin panelling
27. Downward identification lights, red, green and amber
28. Starboard navigation light
29. Starboard aileron
30. Aileron trim tab
31. Aileron hinge control, cable actuated
32. Ammunition magazine, 270-rounds per gun, outboard pair
33. Ammunition magazine, 400-rounds for inboard gun
34. Starboard plain flap
35. Starboard wing fuel tank
36. Engine bay armoured rear bulkhead
37. Hydraulic reservoir
38. Instrument panel
39. Rudder pedals
40. Fuel selector panel
41. Cockpit floor panel
43. Wing front spar bolted attachment joint
44. Three-axis trim control wheels
45. engine throttle and propeller control quadrant
46. Control column
47. Instrument panel shroud
48. K14A gunsight
49. Armoured glass windscreen panel
50. Aft sliding cockpit canopy cover
51. Headrest
52. Pilot's seat
53. Canopy latch
54. Flare launcher
55. Adjustable seat mounting
56. Oil and coolant radiator shutter controls
57. Wing rear spar bolted attachment joint
58. Fuselage self-sealing bag-type fuel cell, capacity 70.8 Imp gal (85 US gal, 321 lit)
59. Fuselage fuel tank filler cap
64. Dust proof bulkhead
65. Sliding canopy rail
66. Type F2 low pressure oxygen cylinders (2)
67. Antenna mast
68. D/F loop antenna
69. Fin root fillet
70. Tailplane bolted attachment joints
71. Fin front spar joint
72. Elevator control links, cable actuated
73. Starboard tailplane

74. Fabric-covered elevator
75. Phenolic resin trim tab, all positions
76. HF antenna cable
77. Rudder trim tab actuator
78. Two-spar and rib fin structure
79. Rudder mass balance
80. Rudder trim tab
81. Fabric-covered elevator rib structure
85. Elevator mass balance

86. Elevator tab actuator
87. Two-spar and rib tailplane structure, continuous tip-to-tip
88. rudder hinge control link
89. Tailplane spar mounting bulkheads
90. Tailwheel retraction jack
91. Tailwheel doors
92. Steerable tailwheel
93. Tailwheel shock absorber leg strut

94. Tail assembly attaching bulkhead
95. Fuselage lifting bar
96. Radiator shutter hydraulic actuator
97. D/F equipment rack
98. Type D2 low pressure oxygen cylinders
99. Oxygen filler point
100. Coolant radiator air shutter
101. Radiator exhaust duct
102. Coolant radiator
103. Wing root trailing edge fillet
104. Oil cooler shutter control jack
105. Position of flap hydraulic jack on starboard side
106. Flap actuating link and interconnecting torque shaft
107. Ventral oil cooler

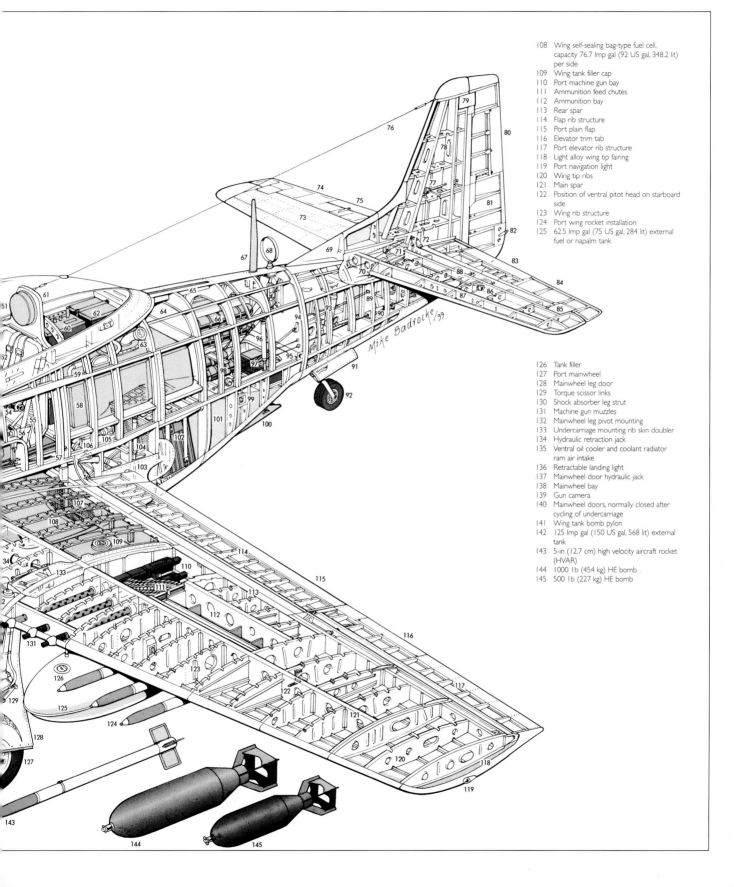

108 Wing self-sealing bag-type fuel cell, capacity 76.7 Imp gal (92 US gal, 348.2 lit) per side
109 Wing tank filler cap
110 Port machine gun bay
111 Ammunition feed chutes
112 Ammunition bay
113 Rear spar
114 Flap rib structure
115 Port plain flap
116 Elevator trim tab
117 Port elevator rib structure
118 Light alloy wing tip fairing
119 Port navigation light
120 Wing tip ribs
121 Main spar
122 Position of ventral pitot head on starboard side
123 Wing rib structure
124 Port wing rocket installation
125 62.5 Imp gal (75 US gal, 284 lit) external fuel or napalm tank

126 Tank filler
127 Port mainwheel
128 Mainwheel leg door
129 Torque scissor links
130 Shock absorber leg strut
131 Machine gun muzzles
132 Mainwheel leg pivot mounting
133 Undercarriage mounting rib skin doubler
134 Hydraulic retraction jack
135 Ventral oil cooler and coolant radiator ram air intake
136 Retractable landing light
137 Mainwheel door hydraulic jack
138 Mainwheel bay
139 Gun camera
140 Mainwheel doors, normally closed after cycling of undercarriage
141 Wing tank bomb pylon
142 125 Imp gal (150 US gal, 568 lit) external tank
143 5-in (12.7 cm) high velocity aircraft rocket (HVAR)
144 1000 lb (454 kg) HE bomb
145 500 lb (227 kg) HE bomb

Mike Badrocke/99

F-51 Mustang Patch Gallery